BE THE BEST

*A Focus on Individual
Responsibility for Achieving*

Harvey Alston
Best, Inc.

KENDALL/HUNT PUBLISHING COMPANY
4050 Westmark Drive   Dubuque, Iowa 52002

A guide to finding your career for student Grades 7th through 12th, and for teachers and parents who give guidance.

BE THE BEST of Whatever You Are

If you can't be a pine on the top of the hill,
 Be a scrub in the valley—but be
The best little scrub by the side of the rill;
 Be a bush if you can't be a tree.

If you can't be a bush, be a bit of the grass,
 Some highway happier make;
If you can't be a muskie, then just be a bass—
 But the liveliest bass in the lake!

We can't all be captains, we've got to be crew,
 There's something for all of us here,
There's big work to do, and there's lesser to do,
 And the task we must do is the near.

If you can't be a highway, then just be a trail,
 If you can't be the sun, be a star;
It isn't by size that you win or you fail—
 Be the best of whatever you are!

Douglas Malloch

Dedication to My Father

Harvey H. Alston, Sr.

My father was one out of six children born to a North Carolina farmer. He was brought into the world in a small house in Graham, North Carolina, August 24, 1906. After the family moved to Columbus, Ohio in May of 1913, he entered Champion Elementary School and graduated from East High School in 1925.

In 1931, Harvey decided he wanted to be a policeman and took the test. Even though he placed 11th on the examination, it was not until six years later that they would accept another African American on the force. In 1937, he became the 12th African American on the force. In October, 1946, he was the first African American promoted to Sergeant. In 1952, he was the first African American promoted to Captain. In 1954, he was promoted to Inspector of Police, the highest ranking African American in the country.

Dad was best known for his accomplishments with youth. Not only did he serve as a Lieutenant of the police, where he ran the Juvenile Bureau, but in 1950, he also served on the "National White House Conference on Youth" under President Truman. Then in 1952, he served on the Kefauver Commission. During his command, the Columbus Police Department was recognized as one of the leading authorities on juvenile problems.

Later in his career as Sergeant Major of the Ohio National Guard "African American Unit", he organized the Company B and 372nd anti-aircraft artillery mobile weapons unit.

My father had many awards, but nothing he did in his life meant as much to me as the fact that no one ever said he was unfair, no one ever said he was playing around with women, and no one ever saw him drink, or chew. He had faults, but they were few. He was a strong, black man, supported and held up by a strong, black woman, and together they made their mark on life.

Contents

PHASE ONE: Market Yourself, 1

You are the best product you have. Become consumed with selling you.

PHASE TWO: What Do You Love?, 17

Become aggressive in discussing what you love. Pursue that goal.

PHASE THREE: What You See is What You Get, 27

See yourself not as you are, but rather as you would like to be.

PHASE FOUR: Find a Star and Hook Your Wagon, 35

Find people who are successful at what you like. Copy them and study them.

PHASE FIVE: Go for the Goals, 47

Let's make some plans.

PHASE SIX: Self Development, 55

It doesn't cost very much. Build your mind.

PHASE SEVEN: Looking Glass, 63

We judge books by the cover. Put on the right jacket.

PHASE EIGHT: Get Involved, 73

Become the hub, not the spoke. Today the squeaky wheel gets replaced.

PHASE NINE: Work Ethic, 79

How much do you want? How hard are you willing to work?

PHASE TEN: Fitness, 99

Mind, body and soul. Your body is the instrument you use to express your talents. Is it tuned?

Completion of Phases, 115

BE THE BEST - Be H.A.P.P.Y.

Foreword

Only a few times in your life do you come in contact with someone who is the ultimate "doer." Harvey Alston is one of those rare people. I have had the opportunity to work with, consult with and know over 2000 people who are speakers, authors, consultants, athletes, businesspeople or educators. I can count on one hand the number who fall in the category of an absolute "doer". There are some people who talk about one thing, yet do the other. Harvey does what he talks about. There is no hypocrisy, in any way. When he makes up his mind to accomplish something, he does it . . . no excuses . . . nothing stands in his way. He is the most disciplined person I have ever known.

In 1980 when I was president of the National Speakers Association, I said to myself that now I can finish the book I have been working on. Since then, I have co-authored two books, yet never finished "the" book. Harvey started talking about his book a few months ago. Now, it is already reality. That is Harvey's style.

Harvey has an uncanny ability to know what to do that is "right". He realizes that all good things come back to him, many times over, by doing the "right" things. Since he is in so much demand as a speaker, he has to turn down many speeches. He realizes that when that happens and he must tell the client he can't do the speech because he is already "booked", he has a choice as to what to do to help the client. He can leave them "hanging" or he can refer them to someone who can help them. He, invariably, refers them to someone who can help them . . . oftentimes, that becomes our company. We are grateful. More importantly, however, is the fact that he knows that by helping the client, they will remember him the next time and he feels good about not leaving them without having a source for their speaker this time.

Be assured, that if you get to meet Harvey, you will know, quickly, that what he says in this book is his life, his gut, his beliefs and how he lives. It can help virtually anyone who reads it and applies it. Remember the old saying, "It isn't what we read, see or hear that makes a difference in our lives . . . It is what we do with that information." Read this book and do something with the material to improve your life.

MIKE FRANK, C.S.P., C.P.A.E.

Note: Mike Frank has been in the field of speaking and training since 1966. He has received a the top awards from the National Speakers Association, has spoken to over 3000 groups and is President of Speakers Unlimited, one of America's premier speakers bureaus, located in Columbus, Ohio.

Preface

What Is the Cost Of Ignorance

There are over one million people in jail today in the United States. That is more than those who died to save our country in the Civil War, World War I, World War II, or the Korean and Vietnam Wars, at the cost of over thirteen billion dollars a year of our tax dollars.

Juvenile crime hit an all time high of 1.8 million crimes committed by those under 18 years of age, and at a cost of one-hundred seventy-five billion dollars a year on treatment, court, and related costs.

It costs an average of $27,000 per year to house an inmate. At that cost, you could send them away to college, buy books, rent an apartment, buy a car, pay insurance, and still have money left.

It Costs Less to Train People Than to Jail People

We have good programs. Now we need to give these school programs like Vocational Education, College Readiness, Distributive Education, Career Centers, Jobs for American Graduates, Occupational Work Adjustment, Career Education, and Career Development Program the time and the money to make them more effective.

It Costs Less to Employ Than to Pay Unemployment

Through the above programs and others like them, we can teach job skills that will last a lifetime and help cut unemployment. That is why my book "Be the Best" is a must for people who are trying to find employment and for those who are trying to help. It will help in the development of their employability skill.

Acknowledgments

When I start to say "thanks" to the people who have helped me in so many ways, I am reminded of the story about the many who were cleansed of leprosy and only one returned to say "thanks". I am trying to be the one who says "thanks".

To my wife, Toni, and my two sons, Paul and William, without your love I am nothing.

To my mother, whose strong religious faith in God and her constant prayers have kept His light shining on me. For this alone I am truly blessed.

To my staff, although at times, we may have bitten off more than we can chew, you have always stood by me.

To "Doc", Dr. Charles Flowers, for his constant counsel, and for being my hero.

To my best friend, Bill Rose, who sets new goals for me by being a challenge. Bill is faithfully setting the pace out front so that I have someone to catch up with.

To Mike Frank, of Speakers Unlimited. He has taught me so much about the speaking business, and everyday he lends his advice. His selfless manner of teaching has helped me to build a very professional business. Thanks, Mike.

To Reverend and Mrs. Nelson Crawley for standing by me, and for their support as my family. Sarah and Nelson are my aunt and uncle.

To Roger Browning, who as a supervisor, showed me how to manage people. Roger showed me how to build self-esteem in employees by believing in them.

To Dick and Jean Lowe, of ShowBoat Marine, who started me in boating and let me become a sales representative during the boat shows. Thanks for teaching me sales techniques.

To Robert Wright, who finds a book a month for me to read. Robert is more than an employee, he is part of our family.

To Sharon at Samco Specialties, whose staff has been of great help in the development of our workout gear.

To Ed and his staff at the Inkwell, who work hard to get our newsletters out on time.

To the Balfour Co. and Vincent Petroy, who have supported my program in schools across America.

To Rick at America's Fitness Warehouse, whose support for my fitness program and advice on the right equipment has saved me a lot of money and time.

To Rich, whose help with recreational equipment has given my family many hours of fun together.

To the students and staff of the schools at which I have spoken. You are my inspiration. Your love and appreciation for my work gives me the courage to continue. Your letters brighten my days and lift my heart.

To my audiences everywhere. Without you, there is no me.

To all of those whose paths have met mine, whose lives, if for only a moment, touched mine, I am eternally grateful, for what life has given me, and the opportunity to have known you.

Introduction

Be the Best

It doesn't begin with the words, "Be the Best." It begins with the personal desire, ability and a willingness to discipline ourselves. Although there are thousands of books and tapes on "how to do" a job or make one most people have a problem finding out what it is in life that they were made for. It is difficult trying to find that shoe or glove that fits just right, or the perfect job for their abilities. Be the Best will help the beginner find the path, and the more experienced stay on the right road to happiness and success. Each phase of "Be the Best" will take you through a plan along with evaluations that make it easy to reflect when needed. Each phase will help you learn how to structure your life and master yourself. In the last phase, you will discover an easy way to take your new personal vision and through your physical presence live it. It's time. Let's start with marketing yourself.

Praises for *Be the Best*

By Harvey Alston

"You have inspired a lot of people and I know many Missourians are going to be 'Happy' for a long time."

HARRY A. KUJATH, DIRECTOR
COMMUNITY EDUCATION

"Your delivery style was 'the best' and I know you encourage all young people to be the best they can be!"

EMMETT EARY
STATE ADVISOR
DECA, TEXAS ASSOCIATION

"Your message is also important to me because it provides me with the fortitude to continue my quest to provide a positive influence for leaders of tomorrow."

KIRK J. MCCOY, CHAIRMAN
HOBY/OHIO SOUTH

"You not only hit the right chords, but I believe you awakened the mission, or purpose, that we all hold towards our people, and their potential. I believe you are a true hero! Please keep up your work!"

GLENN W. BUSE
VICE PRESIDENT, HUMAN RESOURCES

"Very touching; dynamic; awesome; good and funny; precise, to the point and lively; most inspiring. Very knowledgeable of teenagers and how they think."

CARMEN R. POUGH, STATE ADVISER
FUTURE HOMEMAKERS OF AMERICA

"The overwhelming message that they received was, 'I can do anything I set my mind to do.' For so many you gave them hope."

DAN HUMPHREY
SUPERVISOR

"You and John the Baptist have much in common. Keep on preparing the way for they who follow."

JAMES D. BOGGS, AIA

▦ PHASE ONE
Market Yourself

You are the best product you have. Be consumed with selling yourself and you will succeed.

A lot of people just don't know how to sell themselves. They don't realize that the only product they have is themselves. When I worked for Wendy's and Ritzy's restaurants in the fast food industry, people would come in for job applications. It always tickled me, because I'd sit back and watch people long before they came up to ask for the application, trying to figure out if this was a person I really wanted to hire. Many times I would have people come in, . . . walk up to the counter, who were not dressed for the part, and not acting the part. For instance, a young man came in with two or three of his young friends. The wrong thing to do if you're coming in for a job. If I only have one job, come in by yourself. Don't drag people with you. He came in with two or three people with him, and a couple of the guys had modern haircuts. The kind with slashes, dots, and dashes. One had rows cut into his eyebrows, another had on three or four earrings, and three or four gold chains along with rings on every finger. They walked up to the counter and said, "You're not hiring are you?" I said, "No, I'm not hiring today, tomorrow, or next week, never." Those guys scared me to death. Because of the *way* they came in, and because of the way they looked on the outside I made a judgement. I judged their character long before they asked for the application. Is this wrong? Yes, it's wrong. But isn't this something most people do? I would say that almost everybody does it. Everybody makes some kind of judgment on the type of person you are, long before you've filled out an application.

Some of your personal marketing techniques have to do with the way you come in and ask for a job. In some instances, even if I didn't have a job available, some people I'd pull to the side and say, "Look, some of the things . . . . you are doing are wrong. You're never going to get a job, not unless you present yourself in the appropriate manner." I'll never forget the time that a young man came into the store. Evidently he had been to McDonald's. Now you have to understand, we are at Wendy's. He came right from McDonald's because he had a McDonald's cup in his hand, as he walked up to the counter and asked for a job application. Immediately I said, "Well, son, here's the application, but if you've got a minute I'd like to talk to you." I pulled him over to the side and said, "when you go to apply for a job, you don't go in a person's store with products from a competing store and ask for a job. That would be like someone wanting a job at a department store coming in with a bag full of things from it's competition. There you are standing asking the people at the store for an application. The guy's going to look down at your bag and thinks 'you don't even like my products.' He may give you the application, but he may not tell you why he's not going to hire you. Right away, you've made a potential employer angry. What you have to do is look at yourself, see what you're doing, and then be able to change some of those aspects so you can get a job."

Many times I have seen people come in a restaurant during busy hours, like lunch time, or dinner time, when we would have people lined up outside the door, come through the line and ask, "Can I get an application?" "Sure you can get one. But, I'm not going to be able to talk to you now. I'm not going to be able to deal with you." As employers we grudgingly give this person an application because they're preventing us from dealing with business and from making money.

Another example, a person comes in and asks for an application, and then they say, "Give me two - I'm getting one for a friend of mine." You mean your friend is so lazy that he can't come down and get an application on his own? Well, right away this is someone that I don't want to deal with, and I don't want to give an application to for a job, because he is too lazy to come down and get one for himself.

After having several people do these kinds of things, I've tried to figure out—*who* is the person that really catches my attention and what style do they have that I really appreciate?

I remember one day I was talking to some of the other managers . . . during a slow period of time and a person came in. He had on a shirt, and tie, as he walked up to the counter and said, "Excuse me, sir, is it possible, if you are not too busy could I get an application?" I was astonished. Of all the other applicants who had done everything absolutely wrong, this persons polished approach politely took me off guard. I got this person an application right away and as I handed it to him he stated, "Well, do you want me to fill it out now, or take it home and fill it out? I can do either one." His politeness was so great that I said, "Have a seat." Then he said, "If you have time after I fill it out, can you talk to me, or I'll leave a number and you can call me." I said, "I'll make time to talk to you." Because this person was polite, because he was dressed in the appropriate manner, because he looked like the type of employee I'd like to have, I said I'd schedule him an immediate interview. Now, this person could have had the personality of a Jeffrey Daumer, inviting people over for dinner who would end up on the menu, and I would not have known. But, . . . because of his politeness, and because of the way he presented himself, he made me think this is the type of person I want to have for an employee.

You've got to present yourself in a manner so appealing, and so striking, that you make it easy for an employer. . . . .

Raise Your Hand

I remember my first job. I was a big fellow for sixteen years old—one hundred ninety-five pounds, six foot one, (maybe six foot one and a half). I went to apply for a job, and back then they didn't have the fast food restaurants. They had jobs—rough jobs—tough jobs. So, I went down to a apply for a job at the local labor union, The Hod Carrier's Union. At this particular time, the only jobs available for me were African American subservient types of jobs. Like carrying mortar for the building industry, or running a Georgia buggy, those types of things. I went down to the union hall and sat down among a lot of other men. A person came out who a job sheet. He said, "Does anybody here know how to carry hod?" Four or five people raised their hands and they were gone. Another hour went by, and he came out with another listing for jobs. He said, "Does anybody know how to run a Georgia buggy?" Four or five people raised their hands and they were gone. I sat there for another hour. An old man was sitting over in the corner, (I guess his job was to keep the activities going or his job for the day was just to mess with people) looked at me and said, "Boy, you want a job?" I smiled and said, "Sure, I want a job." He lifted his right hand and said, "You've got to learn how to raise your hand." "Raise my hand?" "Yes, raise your hand." He then said, "When they come in here and ask for a job, raise your hand." I said, "Well, isn't this something. All I have to do is raise my hand." The man came back out about a half hour later and said, "Anybody know how to sand hog?" I raised my hand, and said, "I do, I do." When nobody else raised their hand I knew I was in trouble! I ended up working a job digging underground sewage tunnels for the freeways. I had to go down into the ground through a manhole and bulkhead. Outside when it rained, down there underground we were dry. Then when it was dry outside, two or three days later it rained down in the tunnel. What a crazy job! I learned a lot from that experience. I learned that I didn't want to work in a sewage tunnel for the rest of my life. You too can learn a lot of things from different job experiences, but with this job most of all I learned that to get a job, I had to raise my hand. A lot of other people weren't willing to raise their hands.

Bring Your Lunch

Norris Breen, (a man who worked construction for many years, and became like a godfather to me) taught me a number of lessons. I went to apply for a job once, and he asked me, "When you go to apply for a job do you bring your lunch?" I said "No." He said, "Well, you aren't expecting to get a job then are you?" I said, "What do you mean?" He said, "What if they give you a job today? How are you going to eat today if they take you away from here, out somewhere, how are you going to eat?" See, I came looking for a job, but I wasn't ready to work that day. A lot of people do the very same thing. They come for a job, they bring their children with them, or they don't have transportation, or they've got something else to do that afternoon.

For example, once I said to a person that came to apply for a job, "I want you to stick around here for a minute and do the orientation this afternoon." This person turned his head around so I could not see his face or make eye contact, while I heard him say, "Well, I—I—got something I have to do this afternoon. I wasn't planning on getting a job this afternoon." I said, "Then why did you come down here and apply for one?" You've got to be ready in every aspect when you go to apply for a job. You've got to be willing to *raise your hand*, and you've got to *bring your lunch* with you in case you have to stay all day. Be prepared, because what if you do get the job at that moment and that person says, "I want you to stay and do the work today." What are you going to tell them? In reality what you did was you came looking for a job, but you weren't willing to work. Now you've started out with a negative impression. You're already on the wrong foot or no foot at all. That employer may very well send you away and say to you, "I'll call you." You've missed an opportunity.

You have to show employers on your first impression that "I am the best", and "I'm willing to give my all and all." If you're willing to give your all and all, then you'll always have a job. You'll never have to worry about being unemployed. Show people that you're better than the next person. Show people that you really want the job. No matter what the caliber of job, the same principles work whether it's for an executive position, or a job in the fast food industry.

Approach any job prepared. You won't lose. If I were looking for a job on the corporate level, I would go to the office, way before I applied for that job. Because it's important to know what is expected of you before your interview, I'd survey it, check it out, find out who is the boss, and see how the employees are dressed. For example if they are dressed with big fancy ties, you wear a big fancy tie. If they have on nice suits but plain ties, when you go to the job interview, you wear a nice suit and a plain tie. You could also find out where the employees eat lunch. Sit with them and ask them about their job. Find out if they like their job. Ask about the difficulties of their job. Ask them about their pay. Ask them everything you need to know. Then make a little list of what these people do and don't like about their job and the job situation. Now you have the advantage, because you know a lot about the place of work from what the employees have told you. Now you know about the boss, the job, what the employees like about it and what they don't. Maybe during the interview the boss will ask you some questions that would kind of delve into the business. You could then share with him some of your observations. Why not? You don't have anything to lose. You've got everything to gain.

If it's a job you really, really want, then be creative. A man I know who told me about a person who applied for a job. Even though he didn't have any job openings, because his business was running well, he still received an application. This young applicant had sent him some balloons in the form of a "job gram". Attached to this balloon was a card with some information that said, "I can help your business grow. Give me an opportunity to sit down and talk with you and I can show you how we can make some money." The job gram caught his interest in such a fantastic way, that he gave the young man an opportunity. Since then, his business has grown. He's been able to do more business, and the young man created a job market for himself. No matter when you talk to my friend, he is so excited about this new employee . . . he can't stop talking about him.

This young man made a niche for himself because he dared to be different. I say, take the same philosophy. Send some flowers. Send a Candy Gram. Send a Balloon Gram. If you really want a job, along with your resume send something to make that resume stand out as a little bit different. Make yourself notice-able. What do you have to lose? You don't have the job anyway, so you might as well go for it.

Interview

Go for as many job interviews as possible. Even if you don't like the job. Once you've looked over the place, and the people there have given you an outline of the job and some of the parameters, and you then say, I don't want that job. I suggest that you go apply for it anyway. It may turn out that the job description is not really what the job is like, or maybe the person interviewing you for that job may have another job that he didn't advertise. He may even realize that you're not fit for this one job, but better suited for another position. Or, he may have a friend or an associate, (a lot of people don't understand that the people in the job market who do recruiting have conferences and conventions that they attend) who has said, "If you find somebody with these qualifications give me a call." They may have that note right on the corner of their desk, and you may be that person. So, go on and apply for that job and practice. Even if a person doesn't have a job that fits you, or if he thinks you're too qualified, or thinks you are above the type of position that he has at that point, ask the interviewer, "What do you have?" Along with do they have any opportunities, do they know of any other opportunities, can they recommend anyone that you can see, and do they know of other opportunities or positions that they can share with you at this particular time? Then, several days after the interview, what you need to do is write that interviewer a little note saying, "Thanks so much, I really appreciated your time," or "sorry that it didn't turn out like we thought," or "sorry that the job doesn't fit my particular area," but "could you give me some advice? If I had to do the interview over again, could you point some things out to me that you think I could make an improvement on, so that the next time I am interviewed, I can do a better job?" Wow! Maybe this guy will take a little time, write a note, or share some thoughts about annoying things that you were doing in the interview. Maybe he noticed you were constantly twitching or turning your pencil, or you were constantly switching your movement in your chair, or you fumbled through some notes that you had, or maybe you had on a tie that was too flashy. Now this is something that most interviewers won't do—they won't tell you. Today almost every employer is afraid of being sued. No matter how obnoxious you are on the interview, employers will not share some information with you because they are afraid that you will turn around and use their information against them. You have to be the type of person who is willing to say to the employer, "I'm going on down the road, but please help me. Show me where I've done something that is wrong." A good honest person might share some thoughts with you that may help you the next time. So, go to every interview you possibly can, do *the best* you possibly can in those areas, and ask for work.

Create Your Own Job

A young man, who used to be a radio personality on an African American station, came to me and asked me for a job in marketing. I told him, I didn't have a company that had any openings in marketing. I also said that I really didn't know of any larger companies that have openings in just marketing. As I talked to him for a minute, it was clear that all he wanted was this job in marketing. I said,"Son, they just don't have jobs like this. Jobs like this don't just pop up, they're just not sitting there. Have you gone to marketing companies, and did you talk to them?" He said, "Well, yes. They said the same thing you said. People are coming out with degrees in marketing, who can't find jobs, because it's a tight field right now." I said, "Why don't you think about creating a job for yourself in marketing. Let me give you an example." He was unemployed at that time, and told me "I'll take a job in anything. My unemployment benefits have run out and I'll take any job." I said,"Let me show you how to create a job. First, I find you a job in the food industry, and you start out working as an employee. As an employee you show the people how you can increase sales by doing certain little things, and they'll promote you to a shift manager. Then because of your age, and background, you'll probably go right in and become a shift manager. After that you could become a manager of the store. Consider if while you're managing the store you can show people figures that outrun any other store in the area, and you show them how your store can do a better job than anybody else, then you go to them and tell them you want a job in marketing. Because you've proven that your local store marketing techniques have been able to increase sales time and time again. Then they'll have to promote you. When you go back and say you want that job in marketing, they'll give you a job in marketing. They'd be crazy not to. Look at what you've done. You've created an opportunity for yourself. You have proven that you could do the job. Now, if you don't have confidence, don't do it. You'll lose. But, if you have confidence in your greatness, then you can start on any level. In no time at all you will run by other people."

Start at the Bottom

Today you cannot start at the top. It seems that everybody that comes for an interview wants to be the boss. I ask, "What kind of job do you want?" They reply, "I want to be the boss. I want to be in charge of things." If you want to be the boss you have to pay the cost. You have to start at the bottom. One of the great things that I learned through Dave Thomas' Wendy's International program, is that no matter who they hire, they start them out at the bottom. Earl Burton, a former chief of police, was hired to do the security at Wendy's International. What a top notch job! What did he have to do? He had to learn how to wash dishes, sweep floors, and run a cash register. He had to learn how to put food on a salad bar before they let him do the job as head man of security for Wendy's International. Why did they start him at the bottom? Because everybody starts at the bottom. Wendy's International philosophy is that . . . as an employee you have to know and appreciate how the money is made, and it is made by selling hamburgers the good old-fashioned way. Dave Thomas starts all his employees at the store level and they have to work their way up.

I had the great opportunity to work side-by-side with Joe Morgan, the baseball Hall of Famer. He bought some franchises, they brought him in and he had to learn to sweep and mop floor, and how to make a sandwich by turning that hamburger over and putting catsup, mustard, and pickle on the bun. He had to learn how to run the grill, and it was interesting to see him develop an appreciation for others and their jobs because, he had to start at the bottom.

Remember the young man who came to me for the marketing job, and I showed him how to start at the bottom? The examples I told him were the lessons I learned, not because it was written in the book, but because it was "the book". I was giving this young man a chance in life based on experiences.

When I started at Wendy's International I had to learn how to make hamburgers. I also had to learn how to run a cash register. But, I told myself that I was going to learn how to run a cash register better than anybody else. I also developed some techniques for being able to take orders and run a cash register faster than others. Then I learned how to talk to two or three customers, and I taught my people working the register to do the same.

When you start at the bottom then you can teach other people how to do it. My people could hold two or three conversations, ring up orders, and get them correct! It was the same technique that I used when I moved to the Ritzy's restaurant downtown, and eventually we had the fastest customer service possible.

Show the World You Can

I never will forget when I was moved to the Hilliard store. Sales had been average there, but in the first month I had increased total sales by thirty-two percent. The second month, I increased sales by forty-one percent. In the third month, I had increased sales by forty-nine percent! In the fifth month, I increased sales fifty-two percent. In the sixth month I increased sales fifty-five percent. They said, "No way. This is impossible." Then they said, "We're going to move you over to the corporate store, where they have the highest volume." (They thought maybe this was just a fluke at the Hilliard store.) This is where we brought the new trainees and did the training. There was a lot of business at that store. In the first month, we increased sales twelve percent. The second month sales increased twenty-two percent. The third month sales increased thirty-three percent. Was it a fluke? It wasn't a fluke. I had found the way to do marketing in the stores to increase business. I had a track record. I could now go back and pull out records, month after month after month, with congratulations from the corporate office for a job well done, for increasing sales, and for being in the Top Ten each month. No matter what, I was in the Top Ten for something. It wasn't a fluke. I learned how to take something and to do it well.

We all have to start at the bottom, each time, and over and over. No matter what it is you do whether it is taking a restaurant and increasing sales, or anything else you've got to work your way up to the top. Then you don't have to worry about anything. People will come to you. Be inventive.

Light Menu

In one of the stores I managed we came out with a chicken sandwich, and a small salad that was called the "light menu". At that particular time we were trying to offer a variety for people who were more conscious about their weight. We were trying to find some way to do local store marketing that would increase the light menu sales. So, here I am sitting with this light menu, and trying to find a way to advertise and market it. I found out that there was a health and aerobics club not too far away from my restaurant. Women would come in all the time, and eat at the salad bar. They had the aerobics studio down the street and their business was doing okay, but not all that great. I said, "You know, maybe we can help each other. Maybe we can have a business relationship here." So I asked one of the women if she would bring maybe four or five people with her, and the aerobics instructors. "We'll advertise for the light menu, and you can advertise for aerobics. I'll get the newspaper and T.V. station and we'll put some music out here on the front of the lawn. We'll have you do aerobics on the front lawn during lunch for just one day as an advertising gimmick. Let's see how it goes." Well, doggone it, the women came out and had on exercise leotards. They walked right out front, had their aerobic music going, and they started dancing. The cars started lining up, as people watched them go through their routines. It backed up traffic for half a mile. The newspaper and T.V. people came there, and I had my picture taken with the women. I was out in front with my shirt and tie on, and doing aerobics right along with the women. The show hit the paper and people started coming in. I heard things like, "I like that *light menu*". "I saw you in the paper," and "I saw you on television." Later Dave Thomas, the founder, came down to the store, after he saw the article and said, "Hey, that was really sharp!" I got a chance to lift myself up, and it didn't cost me any money. While, the women got a chance to advertise their aerobic center down the street. It was a win-win situation all the way.

This is what you have to look for when you are marketing yourself and looking for a job. Ask questions like, can you win? How can our employer win? What can you do to make things right? Don't forget—you are the only product you have. Don't sell yourself too cheap. Sell yourself for what you're really worth. Believe in yourself, and believe that you can do it. Go out in this world and make a name for yourself.

✎ PHASE ONE EXERCISES

I understand that to be totally employable, I must make some changes. Listed are my top 10.

1.

2.

3.

4.

5.

6.

7.

8.

9.

10.

I know and I feel there are things I can do, right now, better than most people, and here are my *best* top 10.

1.

2.

3.

4.

5.

6.

7.

8.

9.

10.

List the materials you have on selling yourself or self esteem, self image, professional growth.

Books	Tapes	Magazines	Video-cassettes
1.	1.	1.	1.
2.	2.	2.	2.
3.	3.	3.	3.
4.	4.	4.	4.
5.	5.	5.	5.

Newspapers	Radio	Television	Computer Software
1.	1.	1.	1.
2.	2.	2.	2.
3.	3.	3.	3.
4.	4.	4.	4.
5.	5.	5.	5.

Examples:

Books: *Think and Grow Rich; Awaken the Giant Within*

Tapes: *Les Brown*

Magazines:

Videocassettes:

Newspapers:

Radio:

Television:

Computer Software:

▦ PHASE TWO
What Do You Love?

Become aggressive in discovering what you love, pursue that goal, and together this will bring you to success.

Part of trying to figure out what you want to do in life is to be associated with what you love. Anything that you like is so tied in with who you are that it is hard to separate them. We find a lot of people today unsatisfied with jobs, because they just don't like what they are doing. I find people in professions, such as teaching, who can't stand kids. Or people in job positions of doing a lot of paper work who would love to be outdoors. Then there are people outdoors who hate being out in the cold or sunshine, who would rather be inside. There are people who take a job without realizing all the things they really like, or love about themselves, or for what they have a passion about. First of all, we have to develop a philosophy about who we are and what we are about. What we like doing. Then, when we develop a philosophy, everything that we do in this life will have a purpose and meaning. That's what's wrong with us today—sometimes we don't have a purpose and a meaning. I suggest to everyone that they develop a creed, a credo, or a philosophy. A way of life. What do you really believe in? I found one that fits in my personality, and altered it to fit my goals. The Harvey Alston creed is on the next page.

That's my credo. That's my way of life. That's my philosophy. So now everything I do is centered around a credo, a philosophy. I don't want any jobs that don't fit into this purpose, and into my plan of helping people. I don't want anything to go in any other direction or any other field. If somebody offered me a job that wasn't tied to my philosophy, I would say "Thank you for the opportunity, but it's not something I want to do right now."

HARVEY ALSTON'S CREED

I BELIEVE THAT EACH INDIVIDUAL HAS THE RIGHT TO ESTABLISH HIS OR HER OWN CAREER GOALS.

I BELIEVE THAT EACH INDIVIDUAL HAS THE RIGHT TO DEVELOP SKILLS NECESSARY TO ACHIEVE THEIR GOALS.

I BELIEVE THAT A PERSON SHOULD CHOOSE A VOCATION APPROPRIATE TO THEIR INTEREST, ABILITIES AND APTITUDE.

I BELIEVE IN THE SUCCESS OF THE FREE ENTERPRISE SYSTEM.

I BELIEVE THAT BUSINESS, EDUCATION, GOVERNMENT, & COMMUNITY SHOULD BAND TOGETHER TO HELP THE YOUTH OF OUR NATION.

I BELIEVE THAT EACH INDIVIDUAL HAS THE RESPONSIBILITY TO DEVELOP AN APPRECIATION AND RESPECT FOR PRODUCTIVE WORK.

I BELIEVE THAT ALL PERSONS SHOULD HAVE THE OPPORTUNITY TO DEVELOP THEIR POTENTIAL.

I BELIEVE THAT EACH PERSON MUST RECOGNIZE THE CONTRIBUTIONS THEY CAN MAKE TO SOCIETY.

I BELIEVE THAT AN INDIVIDUAL'S SUCCESS IS EARNED THROUGH ONE'S OWN EFFORT.

I BELIEVE THAT SOME OF YOUR GROWTH DEPENDS ON MY ABILITIES AND EXPERIENCES.

THEREFORE, I BELIEVE THAT I CAN HELP YOU BECOME ALL THAT YOU NEED TO BE, BECAUSE I BELIEVE IN YOU.

I've got this goal in mind, this credo, this philosophy, and if it fits in, then that's what I want. What do you like doing? What do you want to do in this world?

People who love things find time to do them. Consider, a guy who's tinkering on a car, or building a project out in the garage and his wife calls him to dinner, he'll say, "I can't come right now." She'll say, "Honey, the food is getting cold." He says "Okay, I'll be there in a minute." Still, he keeps on tinkering, and he doesn't care if the food is cold. When he finally comes in, he doesn't complain about the food being cold. Everything is fine because he did what he wanted to do. He stayed out there working on his project.

People who are entrenched with their jobs, and love what they're doing will bubble over and can't stop talking about what they love doing, because they have found their niche in life. A lot of times people just don't realize what their niches are, and they don't look for the things they really love in a job opportunity or career, that's tied in with what they're doing. No, we end up seeing people doing the same jobs day to day, who can't stand going to work, who can't stand working, and who can't stand being there all day. They count the clock, they count the hours, till they've been there for twenty years and they've got the days counted they have left. Then they say, "I've got four years, nine months, thirty seven days, ten hours to go and then I'm going to retire." They are so miserable that they die right after they retire because, they set that goal. They just stay in there long enough so they can get out of "this hell that I've been in all these years." I'm telling you, if you're living that kind of life you need to get out of it. You need to find something that you like doing, and go ahead and do it. Do it with all your might, and with all that you possibly can. If you really love something, then you won't be like the girl at McDonald's, who said when I drove up to the window, "Yeah, and what do you want?" Well, I knew that was a person that really didn't love her job. I said to her, "I'm sorry, ma'am, I really didn't want anything." I drove on off because I wasn't going to be waited on by a person who was so unhappy.

Discontented Workers

More and more, I've gotten to the point that when I see someone who really doesn't like their job and handles me in a negative manner, I go somewhere else. I don't want to be waited on by somebody negative. I want to be waited on by somebody who likes their job, so I can get what's right, and what I deserve. The least I deserve is a pleasant attitude. I don't deserve to be treated like I have stopped somebody from their work, or that I interrupted their phone call. I have gone from place to place too many times seeing people who just hate their jobs.

So, how can you find a job you like? Sit down and make a list. Put down things like this is what I like, and this is what I like doing. Then go around and see how many jobs that you can find that provide the same opportunity for the excitement, the thrill, and the enjoyment of the things that you like doing. There's nothing more exciting than when I see somebody's eyes light up when they say, "You know, I really like children and I really like working with children." When you see them in a day care center and they really enjoy it. They don't care if they get a raise. They're there because they like what they're doing. If somebody comes along and gives them a raise they are so excited because somebody appreciated their job. It's easy to give a person like that a raise, because they come to work excited, and they leave excited. (You almost have to throw them out and tell them to go home!) When I see a person like that, it just thrills my heart that they found employment that they like.

What do you really like doing? Do you like working at all? If you don't like your job, you'll become one of the "can" persons—come to work as late as you can, sit on your "can", take all you can, leave as early as you can, and make life miserable for as many people as you can.

I travel a lot and I go around speaking to a lot of schools all over the country, and on every Friday, I'm always amazed that around noon or one o'clock, the highway is always crowded. Don't these people work? I thought jobs were nine to five, or eight to four. How can the cars that are lined up bumper to bumper on the highway be going in both directions? I don't care what state you're in, what county, they're always crowded on Fridays. It seems that by three o'clock in the afternoon everybody's taking off. Where's everybody in a hurry to go? I don't want to go anywhere. I want to stay, create, and become better at my job.

Happy Hours

When Saturday morning comes, you'll find me in my office. I am not sleeping late because I was out Friday night. My happy hour is when I can get up and go to work. That's my happy hour. Or, I'm happy to be there and ready to go so I can create something new, a new philosophy, and a way to make more money. When I see people on the highway headed to the happy hour almost ready to run you over, I know they're people not satisfied with their employment and they're trying to find happiness in a glass. At happy hour.

Well, you can't climb the ladder of success in a bottle. You can't climb that ladder of success by staying out late with the buzzards and trying to fly with the eagles the next day. When you love your place of employment, and you like what you're doing, your job becomes your all and all. It blends with your philosophy of life, and you don't have to worry about being successful. Success will come to you. Success will knock on your door. Success will ring your phone. Success will follow you home. A person can only find out what their purpose is, through what they love. Ask yourself; What do you love? What are you set up to be? What is your objective to be reached or accomplished? What is your reason for being? Your aim in life? What is it that you were born to do? Because, what you were born to do is closely tied to what your interests are and what you like. Consider the following:

**When you find out what you love,
You begin to find out who you are.**

**When you find out who you are,
Then you can find out your purpose.**

**When you find out your purpose,
Then your whole life will unfold for you.**

Because everything becomes an objective, everything you do will be tied in with your sole reason for being. So I say to you, again, find out what you love, because this is your nature of being.

✎PHASE TWO EXERCISES

I know there are careers I would do if I could. Here are my top ten.

1.

2.

3.

4.

5.

6.

7.

8.

9.

10.

I love do these top ten more than anything.

1.

2.

3.

4.

5.

6.

7.

8.

9.

10.

Listed below are the things that are on your "I would do" list that are not on your "I love" list.

1.

2.

3.

4.

5.

6.

7.

8.

9.

10.

List the materials you have read on career choice, or on your type of profession.

Books	Tapes	Magazines	Video-cassettes
1.	1.	1.	1.
2.	2.	2.	2.
3.	3.	3.	3.
4.	4.	4.	4.
5.	5.	5.	5.

Newspapers	Radio	Television	Computer Software
1.	1.	1.	1.
2.	2.	2.	2.
3.	3.	3.	3.
4.	4.	4.	4.
5.	5.	5.	5.

Examples:

Books:

Tapes:

Magazines:

Videocassettes:

Newspapers:

Radio:

Television:

Computer Software:

⧈ PHASE THREE
What You See is
What You Get

Visualization or Daydreams

You must be able to visualize your dreams in order to achieve them. Without a plan, without a visualization, everything in life becomes a daydream. Daydreams may be entertaining but they rarely produce results. When most people daydream they jump immediately to where they want to end up or a stage in their life. For instance, somebody who sits back and says they want to be a singer, dream of themselves sitting backstage at a concert, even if they never learned the words to the song or practiced the music to the song. Some, dream of driving a boat on the ocean, dreaming they could be there, but never learning how to stay on course or operate a boat. You must reprogram your mind to achieve a more positive behavior and feeling. If you're overweight, see yourself as a thin person. Start walking and talking like those thin people do and it will start happening. It will help you in your diet. Visualize the things you want. If you want a new job, then see yourself in that job. Plan your next move step by step, and minute by minute. This will build confidence and self esteem when you apply for that position. When you see kids playing basketball on the court, they imitate the better players. They see themselves going to the hoop. They want to be just like Michael Jordan. That is no more than a visualization or rehearsal for them. See yourself as a winner, and you'll be a winner. This is the time to start moving toward those steps of visualization. Keep in mind that if you see yourself as a failure, you'll be a failure. Be careful about those things that you pick, and say that you want. Remember, some people say be careful what you pray for because it might come true. Visualizing the goal is good. We will get to the goal building in another chapter, but we are just going to talk about the visualization of things. Seeing things as you would like them to be.

Yachts of Fun

I tell this story about watching television and seeing Robin Leach's program, *Lifestyles of the Rich and Famous*. My wife and children were sitting around the T.V. watching rich people on yachts, talking about this place off of Captiva Island called South Seas Plantation. These people were driving by in beautiful boats. It was unbelievable. I called my wife and children in and said, "Isn't this great? This looks like a nice place. Let's go there someday and see what it's like." We had a vacation coming and we decided to take off. We had to fly into Fort Myers, Florida, rent a car, go across the causeway and go into the first little island called Sanibel. Then, you went to a place across the causeway called Captiva. There at the end of the causeway, was South Seas Plantation, where the rich and famous go. Willard Scott does the advertisements, so you know it's a pretty high priced place. When we got there, we went for a walk, we went past the yacht club (where the big boats are), and I took my camera out. I was so fascinated by these big yachts that I started taking pictures. This man came out on his yacht, and I said, "Sir, this is a really nice yacht. Is this your yacht? You don't mind if I take some pictures do you?" He said, "Well, certainly." Oh this would be fabulous. I got his name and address and said "I'll send you some pictures of your boat with you standing next to it." (He allowed me to take the pictures and I later sent him some). I said to him, "I'm going to have a boat like that someday." And I guess he kind of chuckled. How many times have people told them they were going to have one of these big objects. When I came back home and started looking around, I started thinking. How can I get a boat like that? I met up with a guy who owned the Showboat Marina in Delaware, Ohio. I went to him and said, "If I came to the boat shows and helped sell some boats, would you give me a commission?" He said, "Sure, we'd be able to do that if you sold some boats." I said, "This would be great." I went back and followed my own philosophy and marketed myself. I told him I could sell boats. Later I went to the boat show wearing this jacket with all kinds of emblems on it, looking like I knew what I was doing. I would talk to people, tell them all about the boats. But because I didn't know anything about them I had to read up on them. Even though I'd never had a boat that size because I kept talking, learning, and finding out things, I began selling people boats. Pretty soon I was able to get a few of those commission checks. Then, I went back to the manager and said, "Sir, I want a boat." He said, "Well, that's a possibility." I said, "Good, I want one at a wholesale price." He kind of laughed it off a little, but he saw things my way. I was able to get my boat. As soon as I got my boat, I took some pictures of it and I sent them to the man down in South Seas Plantation. I said, "I've got a boat just about like yours except for one thing—it's better, because, I've got a whole lot *more* on mine." I have to laugh about that. You have to visualize. You have to dream about things. You have to be able to see them not for what they are but for what they could be. Most people who see things as they are never achieve any more.

I Have a Dream

Great men see things not as they are but as they would like them to be. I'm quite sure if during his time, Martin Luther King would have accepted the plight of the African American and never dreamed that one day his children would be able to go to Funland with other children, or never dreamed his children would be able to sit hand in hand in restaurants in the south and be able to eat; or if he never dreamed for the day, he never would have stood on stage and talked about "I have a dream." Deeply rooted in the American dream, Martin Luther King's dream was a visualization that could be. He saw the world for what we could make of it and the way things should become one day.

Dream Book

I say to all groups of people, you must visualize, know things the way that they are, see things the way you want them to be, and when you are able to do that, then you are on the road to success. I have notebooks, not the kind of notebooks you are thinking of, but a big three ring notebook. In the notebook I started writing the goals that I would like to achieve. I have a notebook on health and fitness, a notebook on boating, and one for my speaking goals. Each of my notebooks are labeled. For the one on boating, I look through magazines, such as *Motor Boat and Sailing, Boating* magazine and see things that I'd like to have, or things I'd like to do. (Sometimes in *Lakeland Boating* magazine, or *Heartland Boating* magazine, they'll show different vacations). I'll take those pages of things I want, cut them out and put them under titles like *Here's a Trip That Maybe One Day I'll Take.* Later, I'll sit down with my family and show them my notebook with the pictures of these places and locations, and say, "Well, you know, we could go there one day. How would you like to do that?" I put my dreams in a notebook in alphabetized categories. For example when I wanted to get a water jet, (called personal water wet jets), I saw a *Polaris* magazine and I started cutting articles out on *all* water jets, and on all the water crafts. I started comparing them, based on which ones I thought were best for my use. Would it be the Yamaha, the Kawasaki, the Polaris, or some other brand. Because, I needed a ski to use for the family and one that I thought would ride best, not for competition, but for enjoyment out on the lake. I decided that the Polaris would be the best choice. Then I cut articles, studied, and learned about the Polaris watercraft. When I thought it was time to get one, I got the right one. Because I liked my choice and because it turned out to be just what I had visualized, I got another one. Now, I have two of those watercraft. These are the kind of things that I cut out and place in my notebook. They are a part of the dream, the visualization that has come true.

In my notebook that I have on body building (I get into that in the fitness section), I've cut out pictures of different weight lifters. I'm six foot two, I weigh 225 pounds, so some of the pictures I cut out are of weight lifters who are my height, and size. I put them in a notebook in a certain section so I can look at their bodies and say, "this is what I'm pushing for." Some of the other people, such as Arnold Schwarzenegger, were too big for what I wanted to do, and are not included. But, they are included in a section of one extreme or the other. When I'm weight lifting, I turn to those articles that people have written on weight control and diet, whatever they do, and I use their advice as a guide. When I visualize, I have a guide for my dream.

Children do it. When we become adults, we forget to do it. I have a fourteen year old and he can't wait until the day he gets his driver's license. He buys these little books for car magazines, or he cuts out pictures in newspapers or magazines. Right now he likes this Ford pickup truck. So he's cutting pictures out and he's put them in a little notebook. He says when he gets to be sixteen this is what he would like to have. So when I see pictures of that particular Ford in the color he likes, I cut them out. Oh, I say "I saw another one over here." I want to encourage him to have those dreams, and to be able to visualize. Later when he's sixteen and he gets his driver's license, he'll have the goals and steps necessary for achieving those dreams.

It's good to have dreams and visualizations of things that you want to have in your life. Whether your dreams are a college education, GED, a physical thing (like a car or boat), something physical you'd like to change about yourself, or anything else, visualize it. Dream it. Write it. Put it down in a notebook. Say that these are the things I'd like to have that I would like to achieve. No matter what it is, once you see it, you can start working toward that dream and making it happen.

Now that you have those visualizations, put down a certain time next to those pictures. Promise yourself that these will become your symbols of achievement. Cut them out, put them on your refrigerator with magnets, and write in a deadline—five years I'd like to have this—five years from now I'd like to have that. Then start planning and making those visualizations become a reality. Don't be afraid to dream. Dreamers often accomplish a lot of things especially when they decide they want to change their dreams into reality. Go for those dreams.

Now that we've talked about the first phase of marketing, and you know that you have a purpose, you can now put the other things under the purpose. Some of the visualizations that you would like to have. Visualizations of potential things. Potential means the possibility, or being of having, can be obtained. Now, the next thing is to put it into action. The first phase is your marketability, the second phase, is your love. Now you have the potential of *obtaining* because you have phase three, visualization.

✎PHASE THREE EXERCISES

List the things you love to do. Now let's dream about doing them as a career.

1.

2.

3.

4.

5.

6.

7.

8.

9.

10.

Now that we have listed some possible careers or choices, list the materials you have on that profession.

Books	Tapes	Magazines	Video-cassettes
1.	1.	1.	1.
2.	2.	2.	2.
3.	3.	3.	3.
4.	4.	4.	4.
5.	5.	5.	5.

Newspapers	Radio	Television	Computer Software
1.	1.	1.	1.
2.	2.	2.	2.
3.	3.	3.	3.
4.	4.	4.	4.
5.	5.	5.	5.

Examples:

Books:

Tapes:

Magazines:

Videocassettes:

Newspapers:

Radio:

Television:

Computer Software:

▦ PHASE FOUR
Find a Star and Hook Your Wagon

Find people who are successful at what you do or what you want to do. Copy them, study them, and learn from them, and you will also be successful.

Find people in life who share your vision. What I mean is find three or four people who have done in life exactly what you want to do, who have a job currently, or who are in a position that matches some of the things that you want to do. You may have to search a little bit, you may have to dig a little, but they are out there.

For example, the first thing you can do if you want to go into business, is to pick up newspapers or magazines. Like *Entrepreneur,* or one that lists the top executives in the world, or some of the other magazines which write about interesting people in business. Or maybe you want to go into sports. Get a sports magazine and read articles about people that have made contributions in that field. Don't limit yourself to just players, but read about people who own a team, managers, and coaches. Find those people and find out as much about them as you can. You can also go and get autobiographies of current people to find out about their philosophy, or read about their life and their goals, or to find out how they have become successful in life. You need to study as many individuals that are in the field, to find out as much as you can.

People Who Love Their Jobs

There is always the possibility of writing to a person. Maybe even give them a call. You could ask them questions, and share a few thoughts. I tell you what, I guarantee you, people will talk to you if you ask for a minute. When I was in the restaurant business, I met Bob Evans. I asked Bob, one question about the business. (He's the founder of the Bob Evans Farms Restaurants, and sausage and breakfast business.) I said, "Bob, tell me a little bit about your business." He started talking, and he went on and on and on. He started talking about the hogs, and when they are slaughtered in the field, the meat has more flavor to it. He said people don't go through the seasons of fattening them up and leaning them. They are pulling them from their mothers before their time when they still have too much baby fat. He told me that's why the store bacon has more fat in it, and is not as thick, as the bacon they use to have. He also said that store sausage does not have good quality. Then he went on about how to feed hogs. I only asked him one question and the man talked for forty-five minutes! I guarantee you, if you find some-body who has a love for what they are doing, even though they may be very successful, and you ask them some decent, honest questions, they'll take some time and talk to you because, they are interested in their business. The key is that they love. They found out what they love and they love their business. That's why they're successful. When you ask them a question, they just give it to you from the heart because it flows.

Ask the Pros

The other day I wanted some information on the Polaris wet jets that I had bought. I came across an article on an individual who races them out in Texas, Mike Flowers. I saw the information and I thought I'd give this guy a call. I called him just to ask a couple questions about the performance of the wet jets. I was having a few technical problems and I thought he could help me solve them. He gave me four pages of information over the phone. Through the mail I also ordered some products from him that he said could make it run better. Later he sent me a couple of packages. I called him back to thank him for the advice and the packages he had given me. Everything worked perfectly. It's unbelievable to think that someone who is featured center page in a magazine would take the time to talk to you. But I didn't call him to ask him how to go into a business, or how to get on the front page of a magazine. He is in business because he is the best at racing that particular kind of watercraft and I called him to ask questions about that watercraft and what I could do to make it better. That was his field, that's what he loved to do. He was so tickled that he talked and talked and talked. It was the most enjoyable conversation I've had over the phone with a business person because he wasn't begrudging. He was so helpful. So energetic. He gave me much information. Even if he couldn't sell me a product, it didn't make any difference. He gave me the information about the timing, spark plugs, and how to set the gap. It was just unbelievable.

Find somebody. Get out a directory, or go through newspaper. Find the people who are the top in their field. Give them a call. Ask them questions. Most people will not turn you down—not anybody who loves what they are doing. If they don't like their job, and don't like what they're doing, they haven't found their love in life, and they won't give you the time of day. Time is more valuable than money. If someone will give you some of their time, it's the biggest thing they can do for you. Because their advice, comments or suggestions may make it fly, and save me hundreds of dollars, trying to read through magazines, trying to find out what's wrong and what might make it work. As a matter of fact, I could have ruined those jet skis if I had put some of the wrong material on them. Because he spent his time with me, he saved me a lot of time and money.

When you ask somebody for help, you have a great opportunity. First of all, you must find a teacher who's willing to teach, just like Mike Flowers was willing to teach. Even though he was not a certified teacher, he was a teacher in his field. As long as somebody is willing to teach, and you are willing to learn, then you are on your way to success by having a mentor. Ask somebody for some of their wisdom. Ask for some of their knowledge. Ask them questions about their future, and how they got where they are. It's hard to learn from personal experiences, but it's easy to learn from other people's personal experiences. You can learn from other people. Learn from what they tried and failed at, so you won't have to try and fail. You'll learn because you've learned from someone who's already gone through all the ropes, someone who has gone through the gauntlet. They'll tell you all of the positives and negatives. Be willing to listen, observe, and keep a pencil in hand. Above all, be willing to listen. If you can't find a person that will give you one on one, or is willing to be a mentor, then read some books. Read all the books you can get. Read about the person in your field that you love doing, and their personal experience.

My youngest son who is fourteen, is a four point student. He wants to be a doctor. So he got the book *Gifted Hands* by Dr. Ben Carson, the brain surgeon. He read it until late one night. I said, "Son, what are you doing?" He said, "I'll go to bed in a minute, but I've got to finish this." He was so interested in Dr. Ben Carson and the accomplishments he had made in life, that he couldn't put the book down. When somebody finds something they like and it's close to their love, they have found something that turns them on. Something they want to do, and reading the book no longer becomes a chore, but becomes something you enjoy doing. Doing the research became great and what did it cost him? It didn't cost him anything. He found all the information he wanted because the book for him was free.

Anything that you want to learn in this life can become free—the knowledge is there. If you find somebody that's in a field you like, sit down and write them. It may only cost you a twenty-nine cent stamp. Tell them that you'd like to be like them one day, or that their life has interested you and that you would like some of their time. Maybe they could even call you? Ask them what's the most convenient time? (If it's long distance, you call them on your dime.) Ask them if you call them at a particular time could they talk to you for a couple of minutes? I guarantee you, those minutes will turn into a forty-five minute or hour phone call if you have some intelligent questions ready. Have some questions ready. Have your pen and pencil ready. Ask that person what books they have read to help them become successful. What magazines did they read? What information can be found? Who taught them the ropes? If this person has a book about them, then get it. If the person they recommend is alive, then you may want to get their phone number and call them. Tell them they have been recommended as a person who changed someone's life around and used all means necessary for being successful. Write someone. Call someone. Use that stamp. Go to the library, check out some books. Some library cards don't cost anything. (I remember they used to be free when I was a youngster.) In some parts of the country they cost a dollar. But, a dollar is a great investment for the value you get when you check books out of the library. Check out every book you can on every topic that is interesting to you. Be sure to read as much of the material that you possibly can, and if there are any questions, then go to the bibliography in those books and find out what they used to compile their information. When you do, then you are on your way to success.

Learn from everybody that you possibly can about your field, about what you want to do. Don't rely on people in school to give you all the education you can possibly get. Formal education is the beginning, or a guide for setting you up for the basic knowledge to find employment somewhere in this life. If you just want to find a job and you don't want to do anything else but a nine-to-five, and work for twenty-five years and then retire, then fine. But, if you really want to be successful, if you want to be a person who changes this world around, if you want to be a person who breaks new barriers and sets new goals, then you are going to have to become a person who is willing to self-educate. The only way you can do that is to read outside material then find a mentor who will help you in your self development. Remember:

You are responsible for your own education.

You are responsible for your own employability.

You are responsible for your own likability.

You are responsible for every aspect of yourself.

So get a mentor. Find someone who will help to educate you.

Mentors, Role Models and Heroes

Mentors, role models and heroes can be different people or all in one. One of my heroes and the one person who made a difference in my life is Dr. Charles E. Flowers. He is affectionately known as "Doc". While in college, I had the rare pleasure of being on the Dean's List. At that time Dr. Flowers was the Dean of Students. My freshman year I made the Dean's List for having a grade point average that would have you thrown out of school. Doc called me into his office and asked me to have a seat. Doc loved people and he knew you had to be fair, friendly, and firm. Obviously, those were the letters I had on my reports - F's.

I started telling Doc all the reasons why my grades were low. "You see, Dr. Flowers, I made varsity football team my freshman year and I am a starter. I try to study, but they make too much noise in the dorm. I am tired when I get in from practice." Doc didn't go for any of this stuff. He tilted his head downward so he could look over the top of his glasses, and said with a long drawl, "W-e-l-l, I don't know about that." In other words, he was telling me "that dog doesn't hunt," or, "you'd better come up with something new." The more I talked, the more he sounded like Ray Charles and the end of each of my sentences he would say "Uh, ha." I didn't know if he was biting the bait or just sniffing it out. When I finished my best line and had given more reasons for outside influences, he stopped me.

"What are you doing Friday and Saturday nights, Harvey?" He was "the man" with my life in his hands. What do you think I was going to say? "I haven't made any plans, Doc." He replied, "Don't." Dr. Flowers had me come over to his house on Friday and Saturday to study and I enjoyed it. Every weekend I looked forward to seeing his children who were about two and four years old. I became a member of his house and he had to buy extra food for me to eat. I would study and keep an eye on the children when they wanted to go out. I studied, washed dishes, changed diapers, and changed my life.

It wasn't the study time in the books that changed my life. It was the fact that somebody loved me and cared whether I made it or not. It was the first time that I was away from my family, my mother and father, and I had found another family. I was a stranger and they took me in. Love heals all wounds. Love removes all pain. Love motivates.

Now almost thirty years later, I still call at least once a month, write once a month, and send gifts. Never forget to love those who love you *first*. If you are lucky to find a teacher, counselor, preacher, or friend that you can hook your wagon to, and they can pull you to a star, don't forget them because they are *HEROES*.

You can be a hero if you learn to pass the love that you have received onto someone.

Each one,

teach one,

reach one.

Heroes

by An Anonymous Student

A hero is someone who is believed to have done something to help or save another person. Heroes don't necessarily have to be fictional characters. They can be normal, everyday people. In my mind Harvey Alston is a hero. He is drug and alcohol free, he loves his family, and he has made many accomplishments in his life. Harvey Alston makes his living speaking to people of all ages as a motivational speaker.

Harvey is a hero because he is trying to promote to kids and adults a drug and alcohol free life. Most people say they promote a drug and alcohol free life, but how do they? Harvey gets out and shares stories and experiences to prove to kids that a drug and alcohol free life is the way to go. One story he tells is about a friend of his who held a party to which Harvey and his wife were invited. Once they were at the party, Harvey realized there were drugs there and told his wife they had to leave. He told his friend who was the host of the party that he would have nothing to do with him and he told them he would never set foot in their house again.

Heroes can be anyone. Someone may be a hero to one person but not to another person. Harvey Alston is a hero in my mind.

People: Role Models

In the space below, name some people you like and what characteristics you see in them.

Role Model:

1. _____

Characteristics:

A. _____

B. _____

C. _____

D._____

E. _____

Role Model:

2. _____

Characteristics:

A. _____

B. _____

C. _____

D. _____

E. _____

Role Model:

3. _____

Characteristics:

A. _____

B. _____

C. _____

D. _____

E. _____

Role Model:

4. _____

Characteristics:

A. _____

B. _____

C. _____

D. _____

E. _____

✎PHASE FOUR EXERCISES

I understand that I can learn from people who had been successful in their careers. Here is my list of the best top ten career people.

1.

2.

3.

4.

5.

6.

7.

8.

9.

10.

List materials that you have on the people in their careers.

Books	Tapes	Magazines	Video-cassettes
1.	1.	1.	1.
2.	2.	2.	2.
3.	3.	3.	3.
4.	4.	4.	4.
5.	5.	5.	5.

Newspapers	Radio	Television	Computer Software
1.	1.	1.	1.
2.	2.	2.	2.
3.	3.	3.	3.
4.	4.	4.	4.
5.	5.	5.	5.

Examples:

Books:

Tapes:

Magazines:

Videocassettes:

Newspapers:

Radio:

Television:

Computer Software:

▦ PHASE FIVE
Go For the Goals

Making Plans

Let's make some plans. Sit down and write some goals, become successful, because you have made your plan. Now you are going to work your plan.

When I talk to people about the dreams in their life, often they relate their ultimate desire to obtain things: cars, clothes, gold chains, and gold things. Goal setting must be a part of your dreams. If you are in search of gold, then fine. But set a course to travel to take you to your ultimate goal, or to your destination. If you have never been down the road of setting goals, then let's make a map.

The first thing to know is where you are going. What is your final destination? Once you have made up your mind about where you are going, you must locate yourself on a map. Then you must draw a line to where you are going. On your map you have checkpoints along the way. These checkpoints will let you know how far you have traveled. How far you have to go, places to stop, to eat, to refresh yourself are all included on your map. If by chance you find yourself on the wrong road, you can check yourself and plan to get back on course. But, what if you start out with no plan, and no map? You find yourself on a lonely, dark road with no markers. Now where do you turn? If you do find someone who can show you directions, how do you know they're the right directions for you? Your goal setting is your road map for life. You make the plan, or the map. Make them like your **life depends on it, because it does.**

Now that you know what your purpose is because you have written that down. Now you know what your potential is, as far as marketing yourself. Because, we talked about the possibilities of having a vision and a dream. Phase Five is going to make demands on you with your goals. You ask yourself, what can I do? Have I done my very best? Could I do anything better if I tried a little harder? To make a demand means to call up, to summons, to make a demand on one's self. When a person is running a race, like a marathon runner, there is a point at which they arrive where they are almost exhausted. Then they make another demand on their body to go on just a little bit further. They know they can run, ten, fifteen, or twenty-five miles, because they have done it before. So, at the end of their five mile mark, they make another demand upon their body. They put forth that extra effort and courage the extra strength they have inside themselves to go forth and reach their goals.

Have you made a demand on yourself as far as your personal goals are concerned? Has the time come that you say, "I think I want to do this." Maybe there is a part of you that climbed off the ladder of success and started going your own way because it was easier to do things that are not difficult. It's easy to go to a party. It's easy to go to a happy hour. Working on your dream demands is a little bit more difficult. But it becomes easier, because after you do it time and time again, you can make a demand on yourself, and you can go ahead and go forth into the world. Setting goals is a must. Anybody who's ever accomplished anything at all in their life, has set some kind of goals for themselves. They have said that this is my task, and what I must do. I know my purpose, my potential. Now I'm going to make a demand on myself.

Friendship Goal Setting

"Challenge" is a term I use to call my friends to a contest. As the old saying goes, "if you can do it, I can do it better." I use the challenge in a constructive manner. Bill Rose, my friend of 16 years, and I have challenged each other to become better in every aspect of our lives.

The first challenge started when we first met as teachers in a high school. Until my arrival, he was the only African American on staff at the high school. During my orientation to this new system, everywhere they would take me in the school someone would say, "Nice to meet you, Mr. Alston. Have you met Mr. Rose?" I didn't know who this Mr. Rose was. I didn't know he was black like me. I was introduced to fifteen people and the same thing kept happening. I thought to myself this Mr. Rose must be a king of this place.

Then it happened I was coming down the hall and this big ex-football player looking black man stood at the end of the hallway. His body was blocking the sunlight and it cast a shadow down to where I was standing. We started walking toward each other like two gunfighters on the street in a made-for-T.V. western. As we reached each other's eyesight, neither one blinked or looked down. It was a challenge from the start. I said, "You must be Mr. Rose," in my deepest voice, and he replied in a lower voice, "Yes, you must be Mr. Alston."

That day was the start of a long and great friendship. We have challenged each other on losing weight. We have challenged each other on the size of our homes, who has the largest. We have challenged each other on the number of cars we've owned and most importantly, we have challenged each other on our professional moves, economic position, and our ability to speak, teach, and motivate, saving lives. Even this book will be a challenge to my best friend to "get off your butt and write one." Greater love hath no man than to help build the life of a friend.

✎PHASE FIVE EXERCISES

Now take your list of things you want and mark them on the plan below.

Example A:

1 Year Goal	= 52 pounds a year
1 Month Goal	= 4 pounds per month
1 Week Goal	= 1 pound per week
Can I do this?	

Example B:

5 Year Goal to Earn	= 1 Million Dollars
1 Year Goal	= 200,000 dollars
1 Month Goal	= 16,666 dollars per month
1 Week Goal	= 3,846 dollars per week
1 Day Goal	= 548 dollars per day
Can I do this?	

5 Year Goal =

1 Year Goal =

1 Month Goal =

1 Week Goal =

1 Day Goal =

Try one more

5 Year Goal =

1 Year Goal =

1 Month Goal =

1 Week Goal =

1 Day Goal =

Make a list of all the things you want in life.

1.

2.

3.

4.

5.

6.

7.

8.

9.

10.

On my list on the objects I have set for my new goals, here are the materials I have.

Books	Tapes	Magazines	Video-cassettes
1.	1.	1.	1.
2.	2.	2.	2.
3.	3.	3.	3.
4.	4.	4.	4.
5.	5.	5.	5.

Newspapers	Radio	Television	Computer Software
1.	1.	1.	1.
2.	2.	2.	2.
3.	3.	3.	3.
4.	4.	4.	4.
5.	5.	5.	5.

Examples:

Books:

Tapes:

Magazines:

Videocassettes:

Newspapers:

Radio:

Television:

Computer Software:

▦ PHASE SIX
Self Development

It doesn't cost very much.

Develop yourself. You are responsible for your own education, you are responsible for your own employability, you are responsible for your own likability, and you are responsible for your own successability.

How do you improve yourself? This is what you must learn how to do, every aspect of your education can be improved. Associate with people who are knowledgeable and people who have progressed. What must one do to increase one's own education? First of all it is *your* responsibility, nobody else's. And I don't care what anybody tells you, they've got all kinds of programs today for any type of problem you have. No matter what the problem, there is a program for it. If you were born with one brother and sister, they've got a program or support group for that. If you were born in the ghettos as an African American, or born as a Native American, or you were born as a Jewish American, there are support groups and programs for whatever race you are. If you were born as a dyslexic, if you were born with seizures, if you were born with eye disease, if you were born with hearing impairment, if you were born with any physical impairment, there is an organization that is made specifically for the problem that you have. There are over five thousand different types of organizations that are actively meeting for people who have different types of problems. If you are divorced, there is a support group. I've seen so many different types of support groups I have to laugh at some of their names. I don't even know how they got the problems. There is a support group out there, to help you find yourself and go on with your life. But, in the end ultimately you are responsible. You must stop blaming other people for your lack of success.

You remember this story. There were only two people in this world, Adam and Eve. Now don't get upset if I make a mistake because I'm not a theologian. There wasn't but one rule—don't mess with that apple! You can live life happily, but don't mess with that apple! The apple was messed with. God came along and said, "Adam, why did you mess with that apple?" And what was his excuse? "It was Eve. She made me do it." And then God asked Eve? "How come you tempted Adam?" She looked around and there was nobody there but that snake. She said "It was that serpent. He made me do it." You see, that's the way life is, and the way life has been for so many people, always looking for some kind of excuse and for some reason for not doing something.

Excuses Are Like Butts, Everybody's Got One and All of Them Stink

Why isn't your homework done? Well, we got in a car accident. Why didn't you hand in your homework? My grandmother threw up on it. My dog ate it. Why didn't you get to work on time? There was an accident. We got caught in traffic. Everybody knows that traffic backs up in the morning, and there's going to be an accident somewhere. If you leave early enough every day, you won't have to worry about getting caught in traffic. Even if you do, you can sit there and listen to the radio because you know you are still going to be there on time. A person that is always cutting it to the last minute, is going to be late. Whose fault is it? Is it the traffic's fault, or it is your fault because you didn't leave early enough. Anything that you try to do today will be your fault, and your fault alone.

I get so fed up when people say, "the white man is holding me back." The white man is holding you back? So, what's new? There is always going to be someone holding you back. If it wasn't the white man, it would be the black man who's in charge. If a Native American was in charge, then he'd be holding you back. If a Jewish person was in charge, they'd hold you back. Somebody's always going to hold you back if you're not succeeding. It doesn't make any difference as to the color of that individual, or who they, are, that's the way life is. There is always going to be someone at the bottom. If you are using the excuse that someone is holding you back, then you'll always be at the bottom. Yes, if the person is in charge is different than you and they take it out on you, because of the color of your skin, or the size of your ears, or the size of your feet, height, tall, small, fat or whatever, so what? What you have to do is to become better at what you're doing than anybody else.

How did my philosophy get started? My mother gave me the philosophy for this program that I'm doing called "**Be the Best.**" She told me life is going to be difficult. People are going to hold you back because of the color of your skin. But if you just go out and do your job better than anybody else, then nobody will be able to stop you. Son, just go out and do your very best. *Be the best.* So that's what we must be in life. Stop accepting excuses for your failure and go out and try to do your job to your very best. Now who is responsible? *You* are responsible. If you dropped out of school, so what? Can't you go back to school? It's never too late. I don't have time. Well, you can read. You can find an hour a day. How many television programs do you watch a day? You can cut out some of those television programs out and get a book. Read a book. If you went to the library and read a book a week on your dream, your vision on what you want to become, in no time at all you'd be climbing the ladder of success. Most people don't read and if they do read, they read books that are not associated with their dreams, or their goals. You've got to be responsible for your own development. Open your eyes. Look at yourself. Say what you are going to become. Go out and do it. Go out and become that person that you know you can become. Now the word for the end of this phase is excellence. You have to be excellent. You have to go out and out do. Excellence—to be better, to surpass others, to be god-like, to expose your potential, to be excellent in whatever you do in this life. So if you want to be a great person then you go out and do great work. That's all it takes. You do it better than anybody else. You will climb to the top, regardless of your disabilities, or inabilities.

Determination

I had a young man come to my restaurant and knock on the door, at seven o'clock in the morning. He knocked and knocked.

We don't even open the restaurant at seven o'clock! I said, "Can I help you son?" He said, "Yes, I'm looking for a job? Are you hiring?" I could tell that he had some small deficiencies, not only in speech but in his mannerisms, so I said, "No sir, we're not hiring at this time. But, if we fire anybody then we'll be looking for people in those areas, for those things to do." He came back the next day, seven o'clock in the morning, knocked on the door. "You fire anybody?" I said, "No I haven't fired anybody? I tell you what, you give me your name, address, telephone number, write it out on a piece of paper, and if we do fire anybody, I'll give you a call." The very next day, the third day in a row, seven o'clock in the morning, here comes this same kid knocking on the door! I said, "What can I do for you?" "Well, I want to know if you called. I wasn't home." "Get on in here son." I gave him a job. Why? Because he was persistent. What else did I know about him? I knew he knew how to show up to work on time. Isn't that something? That's something I can't get other people to do. So I knew I had an employee that could at least get there three or four days in a row at seven o'clock in the morning. If he couldn't out think everybody else, or outwork anybody else, he was going to do an excellent job out doing others because he cared.

There was another young man who asked me for a job at the store. I gave him my phone number and told him to call me back because I was busy at the time. I saw him two days later, and he said, "You know, I tried to call, but they said you were busy." So I said, "I'm going to take this opportunity to talk to you for a minute. If I had owed you two hundred dollars, and you had lent it to me, and you really needed the money like you need money now, and you called and somebody said I was busy, would you just not call back? No, I know you would have called back fifteen minutes later even if they said I was busy. If you thought I was trying to duck you, you would have called back ten minutes later. In fact you'd call back every half hour, and every time you'd get a chance to pick up the phone because you wanted to find me. Then if you knew I was getting ready to close the store at a certain time, you'd come back and wait outside the door, so I'd have to tell you whether I had the money or not. You know that.

"If there was a young lady you saw, and she was the finest young lady you ever saw in your life, and she winked at you, and you knew you had an opportunity to talk to her, or wanted a date, and she gave you her phone number, you'd call her at home. If somebody answered and said she's not there, would you give up and not call back for two days? No, no. You'd ask the questions, "well, when do you think she'll be back?" "Where is she at the present time?" "When would be a good time for me to call back?" You'd call back every hour until you found her because you would not give up, because that's something you want. You don't want this job. If you did, you would have called me back, you would have made sure that you found me. No, I'm not going to give you a job now, because I know you don't really want one. A person who wants something does their very best to try to obtain it. You haven't demonstrated that.

So you see, a lot of times we have excuses for things and they are really our own fault. Other things seem more important. We always find time for the things we want to do that are fun, or enjoyable to us, but when it comes to doing those things that will help us to become better, no, we don't want to do them. We can't find the time. We can't find the time to read, we don't have the time to sit down and write, we don't have the time for self development. We have the time to play around. We have the time to go to happy hour, we have the time to destroy our lives. Let's put that same enthusiasm into making our lives better and we'll climb to the top.

Attitudes

Building a positive attitude begins with you finding the good qualities and understanding where you need to improve. This will help you build a greater you.

What I like about my attitude

_____

_____

_____

_____

What I like about the attitudes of others

_____

_____

_____

_____

What can I do to change my attitude?

_____

_____

_____

_____

How can I help change the attitudes of others around me?

_____

_____

_____

_____

Here is my list of materials on attitudes.

Books	Tapes	Magazines	Video-cassettes
1.	1.	1.	1.
2.	2.	2.	2.
3.	3.	3.	3.
4.	4.	4.	4.
5.	5.	5.	5.

Newspapers	Radio	Television	Computer Software
1.	1.	1.	1.
2.	2.	2.	2.
3.	3.	3.	3.
4.	4.	4.	4.
5.	5.	5.	5.

Examples:

Books:

Tapes:

Magazines:

Videocassettes:

Newspapers:

Radio:

Television:

Computer Software:

▦ PHASE SEVEN
Looking Glass

We judge books by their covers.

Don't we judge people by their cover? Don't we judge them by the way they look? We are all prejudiced to some degree. We all like or dislike people based on the first encounter. Sometimes we harden ourselves to other people without even knowing the reason, but we do judge them. Too many times people sit back and say well this is "my thing", this is how I dress, this is my attire. You shouldn't judge me by the way I look.

Some people came in for job interviews. You could just about sit back and learn everything you need to know. One person came in and wore their hat backwards, and had on those saggy, baggy jeans that came down around their hip. Their underwear was showing. (I call them the "just say no to crack pants" - you need to pull them up.) If a person comes in with boots on, or any type of attire, you can tell a lot about that individual by the type of clothes that they wear especially, if they come into an interview dressed that way. We always judge people by their attire. When I was in school we judged a girl's character by the way she dressed. If a girl came in with a very short dress, and revealing neckline, automatically we thought it was a come on. We draw the same conclusion for the guy who wears jeans so tight that if they had a dime in the pocket you could read the date. Maybe these people are not trying to do that. Deep in their heart they may just like that particular attire. But with any kind of clothes you wear you are sending out some kind of signal or message.

Today we do judge, and so much so, that it has split our society. We have young people that wear the Malcolm X hats, and the Malcolm X t-shirts, or you'll see individuals with a shirt on that has on it an Afro-American-type of saying, such as "I'm black and I'm proud," or "Real men are black,", or "I'm proud of the fatherland," whatever. At the same time, if a white person wears a Confederate flag, "The South lives again," or some other kind of reference to white power, we would automatically assume that they're racist. You automatically assume that this person wants the South revived as we remember it in history books, (i.e. slavery). Well, we do have both types of clothes in school and the young people are separating themselves by dress alone.

When we look into other race-splitting factors like music, different types of cultural classes, and different types of vocabulary, then we really have a problem. In this book I am going to stick with the topic here and talk about the judgments people can make about you because of your outward appearance. It's a funny thing. It doesn't make any difference what you wear, people will make assumptions about you.

Formal Power

I dress up in a tuxedo when I go to a performance. When I first started speaking, I would run in from my restaurant business and stay in my uniform with the jacket that had the Ritzy's emblem on it, go out and speak to schools because I was representing my business. My wife and I went to hear a speaker at a program once, and I was surrounded in the audience by several ladies who were listening to the female speaker who had excellent credentials, and she was a very articulate and brilliant woman. She happened to be wearing some clothing that didn't quite match right, and her shoes were scuffed, and her shoes weren't really color coordinated with her outfit. You must remember that this was a very intelligent lady and she had to travel a lot going to and from different cities. She didn't take care of those details in a manner which one, if they were going out in front of an audience would have taken a little bit more care. I can't help but remember some of the remarks of the ladies behind me, they would say, "Look at that lady, her shoes don't match. She's supposed to know all this information, and she can't even dress properly." They condemned her for her attire. I took that as a note for the next time.

The very next time I went on stage, I had patent leather shoes because I wanted my shoes to be as shiny as possible, and I wore the tuxedo because it is the finest appropriate dress that I could find to wear at that particular time. I also found out that it didn't change my opinion of others, but it changed **my opinion of myself**, and it helped to change people's opinion of me before I even started my program. A lot of times I will walk around the area or room where I am to go on stage, and people will see me dressed in this tuxedo before a business meeting, and the attendees will be in business dress, or some form of casual wear. The first thing that they will say to me, "I didn't know this was a formal affair. If I'd known you were going to dress in such a manner, I would have dressed up." Continuing to make suggestions or fun at the same time, saying that I am over dressed for the occasion. It focuses their attention to my presence, and gives me a sense of professionalism because I've worn attire that makes me stand out. It sets me apart from the others.

I was doing a program for the West Virginia Education Association Back To School In-Service Program. Evidently, the year before, they had had a speaker who had written several books on the topic of education and who was well known. He showed up with a five o'clock shadow, dressed in a golf shirt. All fifteen hundred teachers had shown up dressed professionally for this occasion. Ready to go back to school. Ready for the new year of teaching school and their clothes had a sense of professionalism. When he came out on the stage, it didn't matter what he said. He talked for two hours, and the thing the people remembered was the fact that he was dressed inappropriately. He was not professional in his attire.

One year later, I showed up and I'm doing the opening session for this same fantastic group of teachers in the Charleston, West Virginia convention center. The program started. They read my resume and they talked about all the accolades and awards that I had won. The host who was introducing me then mentioned in his speech, that if you notice, our speaker this year is dressed in a manner to make up for the speaker we had last year.

Doesn't this call your attention to the fact that even though the main speaker last year had written books, and given a fantastic program, the only thing they remembered was that he was dressed inappropriately. I was dressed professionally for that affair.

Mistaken Identity

Sometimes the tuxedo does cause some questions, and sometimes you think people are maligning you, or are being prejudiced to you. If I was one who carried a chip on my shoulder I would have thought so. I was speaking at a teacher's conference for a group of Future Homemakers, and my mode of operation is always to show up very, very early for the affair, to go from person to person with small conversation to find out as much as I can about my clients. It was a banquet. As the people were sitting down to eat, one of the things I like to do a lot of is meander through the audience. I go around to the tables and talk to people and find out about their lives acquiring information that I might use during my speech.

I was moving from table to table, meeting and acquainting myself with people, and never really introducing myself as the speaker, when a lady at a table that I'd not gotten to, said, "Sir, sir, come here for a minute." I said, "Okay." I turned around and proceeded to her table and she said, "Sir, I'm out of salad dressing. Would you please get this table some more salad dressing?" She assumed that I was the head maitre'd because the employees waiting on the tables only had on white shirts with bow ties. I had a jacket with a bow tie and a white shirt which made me look like I ran the place. I had no problem with that. I went into the back and got her some salad dressing and I brought it back out to her as she had ordered.

Now they were ready to start the dinner program and getting ready for the introduction of the speaker. As they were reading my resume, I started moving towards the front and going on stage. I could tell that the lady who mistook me for the maitre'd was very embarrassed. She was turning five shades of red, sinking down into her seat, and it tickled me. I never made mention of this during my speech. That woman had made an assumption. It didn't end there. That was only the first time. I thought that maybe this person had not been out to many banquets, or this person had made an assumption about me being black, or tall.

A year later I found myself in Memphis, Tennessee doing a program, doing the same type of mode of operation. I was meandering through the crowd, watching the people have a good time, and as they were just beginning to read my resume I stepped to the furthermost table in the back. I was apologizing to people for not being able to spend enough time with them, when an African American lady said to me, "Sir, will you get me some rolls for our table?" I said, "I would love to, but I'm running out of time now because they are introducing me" as I ran up on the stage. When I got up on the stage, I asked the people who were waiting on the tables "Would you do me a favor? I was unable to get the rolls for this lady in the back. Would you please make sure she gets a basket of rolls?" I had to laugh about it. So you see, sometimes we carry chips on our shoulders because we think other people assume us to have positions of less dignity because of the color of our skin or our attire. People of our same color make those assumptions about us. I cannot go around carrying a chip on my shoulder.

My attire has caused me to attract attention. Frequently it will happen from place to place where I go. Some people handle it well, while others get embarrassed. Once I was doing a program for a PTA association when one lady from the a large table of guests said, "Oh, the food is really good." I said, "That's nice Ma'am, but I had nothing to do with the food." She said, "I understand, but it's really good." She didn't understand my point. I think she thought I was being humble by saying I had nothing to do with the food. I really had nothing to do with the food! I was the speaker. But she wouldn't accept it when I told her I had nothing to do with the food. After I had left her table, some of the people who had noticed my picture in the program nudged her and said, "You're talking to the wrong person." They started laughing and had a good time. We had a little fun because she stood up and let the audience know that she had made that mistake and apologized. From then on, everybody laughed about it and we had a lot of fun. Assumptions are made because of your attire. If it happens when I'm in a tuxedo, then you know what's going to happen to a person who is not dressed as appropriately for some of those occasions.

Your attire will draw attention to who you are. The tuxedo, or formal attire has worked very positively for me. Sometimes when I have completed a speech in a certain town and I run out and get on an airplane right away and not had an opportunity to change back into a suit or traveling apparel with the tuxedo still on, sometimes the passengers will ask me if I'm getting married. They even ask me who I am, or where I am going. Even the flight attendants will make a lot of comments and ask me where I'm going. Several times, they have bumped me to first class because, they figure I didn't need to ride in coach if I had a tuxedo on. I really was appreciative of the gesture to say the least, but it was not something I expected them to do. It was something they did out of courtesy because they felt good about my attire. They felt good about knowing me, and what I do.

Your attire does draw comments about who you are. It says the same things that a cover of a book does before anybody gets to know you, or before you open your mouth. We must make sure that our attire is appropriate for the situation, and if we are looking for a job or a career and the person has an appropriate clothing, we will more likely consider them for the position.

If I had the opportunity to be interviewed for a job and walked in with a full head of hair, dreadlocks, and an African dashiki, or an African Kente cloth draped around me, going in for an interview, I might cause some people to hesitate or think about giving me a job because they may not be quite sure about where I was coming from. The same thing would happen if a person came into my office with cowboy boots, hat, and a string tie around his neck, standing there with a pinch between the cheek and the gum, looking for a place to spit, and telling me he wanted to be a public speaker and he wanted to work for me. I would have some apprehension about this person. Maybe he could change his attire. Maybe he could take out the pinch between the cheek and the gum, and maybe he could become the most fantastic speaker that ever went up on a stage.

If that first impression that you make causes you to look bad and you feel that you are not the kind of person they want, no matter what you do later to try and change their mind, it becomes pretty hard to go back and change that first impression. The mark that you made will stay with you. Make sure that what you wear is your trademark, that how you dress becomes who you are, and what you are on the inside projects the kind of feeling you want to have on the outside. We do judge people by how they look, and by the way they dress. I'm ashamed of this sometimes, but that's the way life is.

✎PHASE SEVEN EXERCISES

I understand that my appearance is of the utmost importance to my career. I am listing things that I can change.

Covered Under Current Health Plan

1.

2.

3.

4.

5.

Not Covered Under Current Health Plan

1.

2.

3.

4.

5.

Find some materials on the styles, appearance, and clothing that will help you make the right change.

Books	Tapes	Magazines	Video-cassettes
1.	1.	1.	1.
2.	2.	2.	2.
3.	3.	3.	3.
4.	4.	4.	4.
5.	5.	5.	5.

Newspapers	Radio	Television	Computer Software
1.	1.	1.	1.
2.	2.	2.	2.
3.	3.	3.	3.
4.	4.	4.	4.
5.	5.	5.	5.

Examples:

Books:

Tapes:

Magazines:

Videocassettes:

Newspapers:

Radio:

Television:

Computer Software:

⊞ PHASE EIGHT
Get Involved

Become the hub, not a spoke.

I've always believed a person should get involved in every productive aspect of their employment or profession. If you belong to an organization, don't just sit back in the seat. Raise your hand and say "I'll do that." Volunteer for it. Become an active member in your community. Get involved with organizations in the community that are going places and doing worthwhile programs. If you look at their resume, people that are successful belong to several organizations and give their time in service. Not only do they give, they get. When they become a part of a committee, they find out how that committee works. When they become the president, or vice president of an organization, they find out how the Robert's Rules of Order dictate the meeting. When they become the secretary, they find out how to take appropriate notes, and how to communicate with other people in written form so that they understand exactly what happened at these meetings.

In many cases how you spend your spare time dictates your future. If you are committed to a happy hour, leaving work early on Friday going to the bars, and staying out late and getting up late on Saturday, then you are not using your time wisely and to the fulfillment of your needs. If you share yourself with other people, and get involved with other people, then you will definitely be helping yourself to be successful.

When I first started teaching school, I went to a teacher's meeting. It was at the beginning of school. Jack Gibbs was the principal. He was telling teachers about different projects they could do to become involved, and he said, "Who's going to be in charge of . . . ?" I raised my hand. I said "I'll take that senior

class." Somebody asked who would volunteer to take the sophomore class. I also volunteered for the sophomore class. Somebody asked about another committee. I again raised my hand.
Pretty soon there was hardly anything left. They said, "Man, you
must be new here, volunteering for all those things." I said, "Yes,
I can understand that." But I was new, on the bottom. I knew
how the game worked. I knew one thing, it's easy to get rid of
a spoke, but if you take the hub away, you don't have a wheel.

If you become the hub of things, activities, and if they get rid
of you, it will take three or four people to replace you. The
administration won't get rid of you. They know who's doing the
work. They figure if they get rid of you they'll have to hire at
least three or four more people to find somebody to do those
same job functions. They will find money to keep you employed.
It works that way.

How many times have you gone to places and the elected
president was absent. They voted for him in his absence. Or, the
vice president got voted in automatically because he thought if
he was vice president he wouldn't have to do that much work.
Then the president quits the organization and all of a sudden he
becomes president. He ended up in a position that he didn't
really want. That's an opportunity to learn from experience. Get
in there, get involved, get in charge, and pass that baton on to
somebody else.

Now that you have learned from your experience, and now
that you have on your resume, past president of an organization,
or past vice president of an organization, people will start
looking at your resume and looking at the community projects
you've done. The fact that you've always been involved in
activities, involved in charitable groups, and other related organizations, will put you in a position where people are more
willing to give you a job and bring you on board because you
do more than what is necessary to be successful. As a matter of
fact, if you don't get involved in good things, maybe you've
become involved in something bad.

There are a lot of people just have time to waste and they'll
use it for either constructive or destructive means. Believe it or
not but there are some people who sit around, and don't have
anything to do who say "I'll just have one cocktail." They're
watching television, and the next thing you know, they have
become a two or three cocktail person. Now if every day this

person comes in from work and drinks three or four cocktails, then it's eight or nine cocktails, or eight or nine beers this person could secretly or quietly become an alcoholic. Imagine living as he does he comes homes, gets obliterated every night, falls asleep, wakes up, and though he does his job in a decent manner, he never lives up to his full potential. Suppose that instead of not living up to his potential he would get involved in organizations or groups. He can then learn from, and grow through those relationships. Wouldn't it be great, every day, to be around a group of people who were smarter than you? Now every day he would be coming home to knowing that he learned just a little bit more. I guarantee you, when you get involved in organizations, get involved in the kind that a successful people are involved in and will pull you up. In clubs like the Rotarians, a great group of businessmen that meet and share ideas. Or get involved with the Kiwanis. They are a group who meet for lunch in the afternoon or for dinner, and they are a philanthropic club. You'll find a group of successful people there. Get involved with the Lions Club. They do a lot, not only for people who are visually impaired, but just the camaraderie of being around other people who can help you develop your life, help you develop some of your values, help in saving other people's lives, helping those to see. When you come away, and you'll feel better about yourself, and you'll come away with self-esteem because, now you can face the world and say I'm great. You will know that you are making a difference for mankind, and humanity. Now go out there in the world and knock 'em down. We must get involved in our community and in great programs. A person who is not involved is a person who is wasting a lot of time in life.

✎PHASE EIGHT EXERCISES

I understand that by getting involved with organizations in line with my goals, it will help my career. I can make it happen for me. Here is my list of job related or community based organizations to be involved with.

On The Job	*In The Community*
Example: United Way Drive	**Example:** Rotary, Lions, Kiwanis
1.	1.
2.	2.
3.	3.
4.	4.
5.	5.
6.	6.
7.	7.
8.	8.
9.	9.
10.	10.

Here is my list of materials that I have on job related or community based organizations.

Books	Tapes	Magazines	Video-cassettes
1.	1.	1.	1.
2.	2.	2.	2.
3.	3.	3.	3.
4.	4.	4.	4.
5.	5.	5.	5.

Newspapers	Radio	Television	Computer Software
1.	1.	1.	1.
2.	2.	2.	2.
3.	3.	3.	3.
4.	4.	4.	4.
5.	5.	5.	5.

Examples:

Books:

Tapes:

Magazines:

Videocassettes:

Newspapers:

Radio:

Television:

Computer Software:

⚏ PHASE NINE
The Work Ethic

How much do you want, and how hard are you willing to work to get it?

The work ethic is something that is so important to us and yet we've forgotten about it. To hear someone say I'll do the job no matter what the job is. I'll get it done. I'll do it to the best of my ability—the work ethic attitude is almost dead. Now you hear people say, "I don't do windows", or "take this job and shove it." Maybe we ought to change that to "take this job and love it!" If you took this job and loved it there wouldn't be any problem. You would do it and you would do it right. What has happened to our work ethic?

Our work ethic has gone on vacation. There is a group of people who don't come to work on Mondays. A lot of employees try to do that. I know what their reason was. They were at the happy hour on Friday night. They were somewhere on ladies' night. Sunday they were somewhere at an afternoon social. By the time it came to Monday, they didn't feel well. Yeah, if you were partying for fifty-two hours straight, and Monday came around, you wouldn't feel too well either. They try to call in with "I don't feel well." I call it Blue Monday. I take the acronym from the letters, BM, well that's about what it is when you call in on Monday. It's a bunch of BM alright! Because most people can come to work on Monday. Some don't want to come and give that extra effort. They've been out partying.

We've got another group of people who expand that group to Friday. They say "I'm getting ready for this party and I can't come in until Monday." The acronym for that is called TGIF - Thank God It's Friday. You hear people reciting those words all over the country. They come to work on Monday, and what are they looking forward to? They are looking forward to Friday! They come in the door on Monday, and say "I'll sure be glad when Friday gets here." When Friday finally gets there, they say "Oh, I can't wait till three o'clock or until four o'clock when work is over." Some leave early, sneak out the door, or call off sick, saying they have a doctor's appointment. They say that something happened to their family, to one of their children, or they have to pick up a child at school. It seems like we are letting these people off, all around the country, to take care of those supposedly important things. What are they doing? They are getting ready for Friday.

We've got the third group of people. The SHIT group - Sure Happy It's Thursday. They get wound up for Friday, and start taking off a little early since they know they've got Friday off, and Saturday and Sunday. They have their weekend three day party time and come back on Monday. Maybe.

It's so contagious that some people started a slogan in the automobile industry that has devastated America for car sales. Somebody passed a rumor around. You want to buy a good car? Don't get one that was made on Monday or Friday. People came to work drunk, they were out playing around. Buy one that was made on Wednesday, because they really get serious about that production date. So they passed that rumor around about American cars. People stopped buying cars that were made on Mondays or Fridays, and on Tuesday and Thursday. They stopped buying the cars altogether, because they found out the cars were not being put together with the quality, or by people who were concerned about their work. The letters *F-O-R-D* used to stand for quality. Now people make jokes about it like;

Found On The Road Dead,

Fix Or Repair Daily, or

Flip Over and Read Directions.

No, we've got to put the hard work back where it belongs. We've got to start doing our job to the best of our ability. We are not working as hard as we can to make that product the *best* that we can. We must do our jobs so well that nobody dead, living, or unborn could say that we could have done that job any better.

What is worthwhile,
Is worth doing.
What's worth doing
Is worth doing it right!

Personal Responsibility in Developing Excellence
Pride

I will work every day in every way to become better and better. If I expect success, I will achieve it. I will use the following time frame as a guide. My *first half* of a day:

Week 1

6:00 a.m. _____

7:00 a.m. _____

8:00 a.m. _____

9:00 a.m. _____

10:00 a.m. _____

11:00 a.m. _____

12:00 noon _____

1:00 p.m. _____

2:00 p.m. _____

3:00 p.m. _____

4:00 p.m. _____

5:00 p.m. _____

6:00 p.m. _____

7:00 p.m. _____

8:00 p.m. _____

9:00 p.m. _____

10:00 p.m. _____

11:00 p.m. _____

Midnight _____

My daily goals from Phase Five Exercises:

1.

2.

3.

4.

5.

Personal Responsibility in Developing Excellence
Pride

I will work every day in every way to become better and better. If I expect success, I will achieve it. I will use the following time frame as a guide. My *second half* of a day:

Week 1

6:00 a.m. _____

7:00 a.m. _____

8:00 a.m. _____

9:00 a.m. _____

10:00 a.m. _____

11:00 a.m. _____

12:00 noon _____

1:00 p.m. _____

2:00 p.m. _____

3:00 p.m. _____

4:00 p.m. _____

5:00 p.m. _____

6:00 p.m. _____

7:00 p.m. _____

8:00 p.m. _____

9:00 p.m. _____

10:00 p.m. _____

11:00 p.m. _____

Midnight _____

My daily goals from Phase Five Exercises:

1.

2.

3.

4.

5.

Personal Responsibility in Developing Excellence
Pride

I will work every day in every way to become better and better. If I expect success, I will achieve it. I will use the following time frame as a guide. My *third half* of a day:

Week 1

6:00 a.m. _____

7:00 a.m. _____

8:00 a.m. _____

9:00 a.m. _____

10:00 a.m. _____

11:00 a.m. _____

12:00 noon _____

1:00 p.m. _____

2:00 p.m. _____

3:00 p.m. _____

4:00 p.m. _____

5:00 p.m. _____

6:00 p.m. _____

7:00 p.m. _____

8:00 p.m. _____

9:00 p.m. _____

10:00 p.m. _____

11:00 p.m. _____

Midnight _____

My daily goals from Phase Five Exercises:
1.

2.

3.

4.

5.

Personal Responsibility in Developing Excellence
Pride

I will work every day in every way to become better and better.
If I expect success, I will achieve it. I will use the following time
frame as a guide. My *fourth half* of a day:

Week 1

6:00 a.m. _____

7:00 a.m. _____

8:00 a.m. _____

9:00 a.m. _____

10:00 a.m. _____

11:00 a.m. _____

12:00 noon _____

1:00 p.m. _____

2:00 p.m. _____

3:00 p.m. _____

4:00 p.m. _____

5:00 p.m. _____

6:00 p.m. _____

7:00 p.m. _____

8:00 p.m. _____

9:00 p.m. _____

10:00 p.m. _____

11:00 p.m. _____

Midnight _____

My daily goals from Phase Five Exercises:
1.

2.

3.

4.

5.

Personal Responsibility in Developing Excellence
Pride

I will work every day in every way to become better and better. If I expect success, I will achieve it. I will use the following time frame as a guide. My *fifth half* of a day:

Week 1

6:00 a.m. _____

7:00 a.m. _____

8:00 a.m. _____

9:00 a.m. _____

10:00 a.m. _____

11:00 a.m. _____

12:00 noon _____

1:00 p.m. _____

2:00 p.m. _____

3:00 p.m. _____

4:00 p.m. _____

5:00 p.m. _____

6:00 p.m. _____

7:00 p.m. _____

8:00 p.m. _____

9:00 p.m. _____

10:00 p.m. _____

11:00 p.m. _____

Midnight _____

My daily goals from Phase Five Exercises:
1.

2.

3.

4.

5.

Personal Responsibility in Developing Excellence
Pride

I will work every day in every way to become better and better.
If I expect success, I will achieve it. I will use the following time
frame as a guide. My *six half* of a day:

Week 1

6:00 a.m. _____

7:00 a.m. _____

8:00 a.m. _____

9:00 a.m. _____

10:00 a.m. _____

11:00 a.m. _____

12:00 noon _____

1:00 p.m. _____

2:00 p.m. _____

3:00 p.m. _____

4:00 p.m. _____

5:00 p.m. _____

6:00 p.m. _____

7:00 p.m. _____

8:00 p.m. _____

9:00 p.m. _____

10:00 p.m. _____

11:00 p.m. _____

Midnight _____

My daily goals from Phase Five Exercises:
1.

2.

3.

4.

5.

Personal Responsibility in Developing Excellence
Pride

I will work every day in every way to become better and better. If I expect success, I will achieve it. I will use the following time frame as a guide. My *seventh half* of a day:

Week 1

6:00 a.m. _____

7:00 a.m. _____

8:00 a.m. _____

9:00 a.m. _____

10:00 a.m. _____

11:00 a.m. _____

12:00 noon _____

1:00 p.m. _____

2:00 p.m. _____

3:00 p.m. _____

4:00 p.m. _____

5:00 p.m. _____

6:00 p.m. _____

7:00 p.m. _____

8:00 p.m. _____

9:00 p.m. _____

10:00 p.m. _____

11:00 p.m. _____

Midnight _____

My daily goals from Phase Five Exercises:
1.

2.

3.

4.

5.

Here is my list of materials that I have read, listed, cut, pasted, viewed and understand. And now I have this information in my personal library.

Books	Tapes	Magazines	Video-cassettes
1.	1.	1.	1.
2.	2.	2.	2.
3.	3.	3.	3.
4.	4.	4.	4.
5.	5.	5.	5.

Newspapers	Radio	Television	Computer Software
1.	1.	1.	1.
2.	2.	2.	2.
3.	3.	3.	3.
4.	4.	4.	4.
5.	5.	5.	5.

Examples:

Books:

Tapes:

Magazines:

Videocassettes:

Newspapers:

Radio:

Television:

Computer Software:

⊞ PHASE TEN
Fitness

Mind, Body and Soul.

In the fitness phase, you must become fit to know yourself. You must be in the best physical shape that you possibly can. There are things that you cannot change in this life and things that you can change. Fitness, outward appearance and fitness of the mind are things that you can change. Let's talk about the fitness level.

When I speak to people about their career choices, and what they want to do in life, some people think you just can wave a magic wand, or give them a formula that will set them apart from anyone else and make them successful. It just doesn't work that way.

Once I was speaking in Alabama, and after the program was over, some people started talking about a young gentleman. They said he was doing a good job and they loved the way he moved through the company. All the people said that his personality was just great. They also talked about how nice this person was. The company then asked me to give him a little personal motivation. So I sat down with him for lunch and we talked. He was an excellent person, and people were right, he was friendly. I kept wondering why he wasn't moving up the ladder of success. He was wondering why he wasn't moving up the ladder of success. Then I looked at him from a distance, and made some notes. The notes that I made were on physical appearance alone. Here's a man that worked for a corporation that would have paid ninety percent of his dental fees yet he had teeth that were missing. This was noticeable and when he ate he was very careful not to open his mouth very full. When he spoke to you, he tried to cover some of his expressions or not grin to the fullest. When we made him laugh or said something that was funny, he would open his mouth and you could see the gaping areas or holes that were there from the several teeth that were missing. I also noticed that he was overweight, maybe to a maximum to fifty or sixty pounds for his size and height. Most of that weight was in the center, about the midriff. After we talked about his success and career path, I asked him could I speak to him privately as an individual that was concerned about his future: I pulled him to the side and we talked. The first thing I told him was that because the people at the top looked professional, and they gave a great representation of the company, if he wanted to climb the ladder of success, he could get his teeth fixed. Why hadn't he done it? I told him he could go get a bridge made, or have a permanent replacement made of his teeth. Then he'd be able to smile and feel good about himself. Because some of his teeth were out, other teeth were moving due to the absence of the others. I told him he could either have them filled, bonded, or have them set back up with braces on the inside of his mouth. They won't be able to be seen and . . . can continue to look professional, and carry on a conversation without having to hide his face.

I also made mention of his weight problem. I asked him had he tried going on diets, or what form of weight reduction he used. He said that he liked to cook and gave me the same excuses that other people give. He was big boned. He gained weight easily. All the other things that people tell you who are overweight and won't face the fact that it's their responsibility. I think that sometimes when working with people in classrooms and we put them in positions for success and we tell them that all you have to do is finish this educational level and the world will open this door for you, but we fail to mention that because of some physical or outward appearance (that they can correct), they will have a difficult time finding a job. We don't want to hurt their feelings. Because we haven't hurt their feelings, the individual will never grow to that job or move into a better position.

When I first started teaching at East High School, the principal was Jack Gibbs. There were a lot of times back then when I felt that if I had shaved in the evening to go to a coach's meeting, or to a dinner, that I didn't have to shave in the morning because my beard didn't grow as fast as it does now. But by noon I would have a five o'clock shadow. I thought that was okay. My first year there, by noon when I got a five o'clock shadow, he came to my room, he stopped in and looked at me and said, "Mr. Alston, I'll cover your class while you go shave." Well today, with all the lawyers and lawsuits we have people would get upset, file charges against him. But the man was thinking only of my benefit. I said "Well, I woke up this morning and didn't think it looked that bad, but it didn't look like I had to shave." He looked me right in the eye and he said, "If you thought you had to shave, or you had to think about whether or not you had to shave, then Mr. Alston you should have shaved. There should have been no doubt in your mind. You shouldn't have questioned it for a minute." He was absolutely right. If you question your appearance for one minute, if you question it, or even think it would have any effect on your job, then you need to take care of it.

Any one past the age of eighteen is responsible for the way they look. No matter what it is. Don't tell me you can't change your appearance. I showed my kids an old album I had of Michael Jackson when he was with the Jackson Five. Compare his picture to now, and you can change everything if you want to. Now, I wouldn't go to those extremes. You can have your teeth fixed, lose weight, or work out and gain size. You can do it and it doesn't cost very much at all. But it will help you make a difference in your life. Too many times we've seen people who are overweight, and go to apply for a job, for a secretarial position, and the position is for someone out front, or as a register person, or having them operate in the front line with the customers, and they don't understand why they don't get that job. Or, why somebody puts them back in a cubicle where you don't see them, or back in the stock room. They know that the little cutie pie, or the person with the nice figure is out front making a couple of bucks more hour, with the customers, and the overweight person grudgingly goes to the back, and says this is my lot in life. It isn't your lot in life to be there. Sure, there's always going to be some people who are overweight. Sure, there are always going to be some people who don't live up to that perfect picture of beauty. I'm not saying you have to be five feet seven and look anorexic, and weigh less than one hundred pounds. Those are some goals that are unattainable for lots of us. But you don't have to have the gut that hangs down, and you don't have to have the appearance that says I'm sloppy. When you are fat, people look at your figure and think you do sloppy work, and they'll never give you the chance, even though you may be the most intelligent person in the world. You need every break and every opportunity you can get, so we have to be fit, and in control.

One way is to get magazines. The other day I went to the store and looked for books that deal with shaping up. *Muscle Fitness*, *Muscularity*, and *Flex* magazine are all magazines I like. *Muscle Fitness* is more for the professional weight lifters, although there are some good articles in there that I like to read. Another magazine *Men's Fitness*, and *Shape* (for women) have great articles for cooking with low fat. (There is a list of readings which I will write down, to make sure that you have a list).

What I do is cut the article out of magazines. If there is one on biceps, or one on triceps, I cut it out. I have a book that I labeled which contains pictures of the upper body: biceps, triceps, pectorals, deltoids, abdominals. Then the lower parts: legs, thighs, calf muscles. All of these muscles need to be worked out in order for you to grow and keep in good physical shape. You don't have to get a membership to a fantastic spa (though a Scandinavian Spa or Gold's Gym, are excellent facilities for belong to). If you feel you don't have the money or the time to go to a gym, all you need to do is get down on the floor. Do twenty-five sit ups. Do crunch sit ups. Do some repetitions of twenty-five push ups with your arms then alternate the position of your arms to gain strength. The sit ups, push ups, and crunches are something that everybody can do and right there on the floor! Roll out of the bed in the morning and do a few stretch exercises.

If you want to do some body sculpturing, inexpensively, get a set of dumbbells, with the weight you feel is comfortable. If you haven't worked out before, I suggest a ten pound set of dumbbells. It doesn't cost very much at all. With dumbbells you can exercise every part of your body that you need. You can do curls for your biceps; extensions for your triceps. From the floor you can do the chest movements. Every type of movement that you can think of, you can do with just one set of dumbbells.

Look at the *gift giving* aspect. If you get one set of dumbbells, and you begin to work out, your loved one will know that you're trying to get in shape. Then when your birthday rolls around, you can get a heavier set. Next you can get a bench to work out on. Make sure you get good equipment—equipment that has the ability to expand. You get a bench, and add on the leg portion, or preacher bench to help in the exercise movement. There are a lot of things you can put together. A complete package that will make everything work (so you can become totally fit) doesn't cost very much at all.

Staying in the best physical shape possible can add longevity to your life. If you're not drinking, not smoking, working out and exercising at least thirty minutes a day; unless you get run over by a train, bus, or hit in a drive by shooting, you'll probably live a long and healthy productive life. But you must work out. You must get into shape. You must take care of those things that you are responsible for. If you're not fit, don't blame anybody or anything but yourself.

✎PHASE TEN EXERCISES

LIFESTYLE

What activities do you participate in that would make you healthy?

Examples:

1. Swim   1.

2. Take a walk.   2.

3. Bicycling   3.

4. Tennis   4.

5. Golf   5.

6. Boating   6.

7.   7.

8.   8.

9.   9.

10.   10.

What activities are you doing that are not healthy?

Examples:

1. Drugs and alcohol   1.

2. Smoking   2.

3. Chew - smokeless tobacco   3.

4. Out late at night (lack of sleep) 4.

5. Late night pizza   5.

6.   6.

7.   7.

8.   8.

9.   9.

10.   10.

My first 30 days of healthy living for the rest of my life.

Today 1st Hour

1st Week:

DAY	TIME OF DAY	ONE-HOUR GOAL OF EXERCISE
Mon.	( )	( )
Tues	( )	( )
Wed.	( )	( )
Thurs.	( )	( )
Fri.	( )	( )
Sat.	( )	( )
Sun.	( )	( )

Examples:

Monday 7 a.m. 25 sit ups

Tuesday 7 a.m. Arm biceps and triceps

Wednesday 7 a.m. 25 push ups

Thursday 7 a.m. Run or walk 1 mile

Friday 7 a.m. 25 sit ups

Saturday 7 a.m. 25 push ups

Sunday 7 a.m. Read articles on body shaping

Check weekly goals.
2nd Week:

DAY	TIME OF DAY	ONE-HOUR GOAL OF EXERCISE
Mon.	( )	( )
Tues	( )	( )
Wed.	( )	( )
Thurs.	( )	( )
Fri.	( )	( )
Sat.	( )	( )
Sun.	( )	( )

Use this check list for 4 weeks.)

3rd Week:

DAY	TIME OF DAY	ONE-HOUR GOAL OF EXERCISE
Mon.	( )	( )
Tues	( )	( )
Wed.	( )	( )
Thurs.	( )	( )
Fri.	( )	( )
Sat.	( )	( )
Sun.	( )	( )

4th Week:

DAY	TIME OF DAY	ONE-HOUR GOAL OF EXERCISE
Mon.	( )	( )
Tues	( )	( )
Wed.	( )	( )
Thurs.	( )	( )
Fri.	( )	( )
Sat.	( )	( )
Sun.	( )	( )

✎PHASE TEN EXERCISES

Here are three (3) essential keys to fitness: Nutrition, Exercise, and Lifestyle.

Nutrition

List the calories you are consuming daily.

	Mon.	Tues.	Wed.	Thurs.	Fri.	Sat.	Sun.
Breakfast							
Lunch							
Dinner							
Extras							
Totals:							
Weekly Totals							

What types of exercises do you do?

	Mon.	Tues.	Wed.	Thurs.	Fri.	Sat.	Sun.
Legs							
Shoulders							
Arms							
Chest							
Stomach/ Abdomen							
Back							

What types of materials do you have on fitness?

Books	Tapes	Magazines	Video-cassettes
1.	1.	1.	1.
2.	2.	2.	2.
3.	3.	3.	3.
4.	4.	4.	4.
5.	5.	5.	5.

Newspapers	Radio	Television	Computer Software
1.	1.	1.	1.
2.	2.	2.	2.
3.	3.	3.	3.
4.	4.	4.	4.
5.	5.	5.	5.

Examples:

Books: *Arnold's Fitness*

Tapes: *Stop the Insanity*

Magazines: *Muscle & Fitness, Powerhouse, Flex, Fitness*

Videocassettes: *Buns of Steel, Jane Fonda*

Newspapers:

Radio:

Television: *Body by Jake, Fitness Pros, Bodies in Motion, Getting Fit*

Computer Software:

The Completion of Phases "Be the Best"— Be H.A.P.P.Y.

Now that you have completed ten phases in the step-by-step program, let's talk about the happy part. This is the phase—be the best—be H.A.P.P.Y. The acronym, H.A.P.P.Y. can be broken down:

The first letter H is for your heart. I already talked about marketing someone who believes in what they are doing. If you believe, and if you love your job, you'll run to work . Every day will be like a holiday. All 365 of them. You'll get up in the morning with the feeling inside your heart that makes you glad you are alive. Other people will see you and they'll wonder what's going on. Your lifestyle will become contagious. Others will think you're on some type of drug because, every day cannot be a holiday for them. But not you. You know the secret in life and that the secret is life. Happiness comes to you and you won't be sad anymore. You've learned to live and do for others. All of these things now lie within your heart, because you have finally found your peace. You are doing something that you truly enjoy. Learn to do your job, and do it from the heart.

The next letter "A", stands for attitude. Attitude will come after you have learned to do something, and do it because you love it. You will then begin to see yourself for who you are. You will be able to see, who, you really are inside. You'll begin to change your attitude. How? You can ask your friends. If you think that you are perfectly all right and have no faults. If you want to know what is wrong with you, ask somebody that doesn't like you very much. Ask your enemies, because your enemies know your faults, and they will tell you. They've studied you. I suggest that you make a list of things you don't like about other people. Write down on the list the characteristics that you don't like. For example if you don't like people who lie, then practice not trying to tell lies. If you don't like people who mislead you, then don't mislead. If you don't like people who are not friendly and courteous, then try to be friendly and courteous to all people. The very same characteristics that you don't like about other people, are the same characteristics that you don't like about yourself. Do we have time to change our attitude? We definitely do! Change it and you'll succeed.

The next letter is "P", stands for people. I get really tired of a lot of people talking all the time that they can't get along with this group of people, or that group of people. So and so doesn't like me, or because they are from a different culture, race, or religion. All of us must learn to get along with each other. Go to a school and ask the kids, "How many of you can't stand somebody who goes to your school?" Ninety percent of the kids will raise their hands. They look at you like you're crazy when you tell them just learn to get along with each other. It starts here. As a nation we're worried about the people in other countries, like Croatia, and Bosnia. We're out trying to solve those problems as well as some of the other people problems that are out there. You can't solve other nations problems, when we've got the same problems here in America. White against Black, Hispanic against Anglo, Protestant against Catholic. It happens everywhere. How are we going to solve them? Can you get along with your neighbors? Can you get along with people you work with on a daily basis? Yes, I know, sometimes it's hard when that person doesn't like you. Wouldn't you rather get rid of an enemy, and make them your friend? Here is how you do it: learn to get along with people. Then we won't have to worry about the world's problems because friendship will spread from your house to the next house. Right on into the neighborhood, and school, then the workplace, and your city, until finally the entire country. It spreads, but it starts with you. Getting along with your family, close relationships, and turning your enemies into friends.

The next letter, "P", stands for pride. Take pride in everything we do. Do you really take pride in everything you do? Do you give it your all in all, or do we as a nation just manufacture something and put it out and say that'll do. How many times have you heard people say, "That'll do." "That will get by." or, "That'll make it, they'll accept it that way." How many times have you turned in homework, or job related work, that was just enough to keep somebody from firing you? We've got to stop that. We've got to have pride. Pride is another acronym, meaning Personally Responsible In Developing Excellence. You must be responsible for developing that excellence inside you. Then at the end of our day you can stand and say "Well done, well done" because nobody could do our job any better because we have done it to the best of our ability.

The last letter is "Y". "Y" stands for everything in these other phases we've already talked about. You. Can *you* make a change in your life? Can *you* set some goals and obtain those goals for yourself? Can *you* start a development program for developing your inner self? Can *you* start developing the "looking glass" syndrome, making sure *you* look the best *you* possibly can in your attire? Can *you* get involved with other activities? Can you develop a work ethic that you will outwork other people. Even if you can't out think them. Can you develop a fitness program that will put you in the best possible physical shape. All of these things are necessary, but they come back to the only letter, "Y", and it stands for you.

HEART: Self esteem—The winner in you, loving what you do.

ATTITUDE: Positive, winning energy, motivation.

PEOPLE: People make the difference; role models, relationships.

PRIDE: Further personal development, work ethic.

YOU: My dream list; visualization, goal-setting.

HAPPY: A personal development program designed for *You*.

Start each day working on your list of achievements. Here is a five day plan called H.A.P.P.Y. Start on a Monday with the first letter and work on your (Heart). Learn to love yourself and the things that you do. Tuesday, (Attitude) is the second day of the week. Focus on your positive attitude. Wednesday, reflect on your role models, and on your relationships with (people). Thursday, is a personal day for development of yourself. Read a book, take a walk, eat good food, take (Pride) in what you do. Friday, cut and paste day. Remove items from your goal list that (you) have achieved, and paste some new ones in their place.

In today's society, people want it all and they want it now. Hard work and commitment, must be a part of the formula for happiness. The great news is, that you have the formula inside you right now. Pick any career you want, and take the first step to making the new and improved you, the real you. The biggest step of all is beginning the process. By starting, you're on the way to the finish line.

So how do you start? Quite simply, pick a goal that you've really wanted to achieve and use the talents that are uniquely yours. Commit yourself to **Be the Best** at that goal, work toward it every single day from "can't see in the morning to can't see at night" until you achieve your goal. You say "It sounds good, I'll start next week." NO! As soon as you put this book down, it's time to get down! "Wait a minute - stop right there!" You have already picked out your first goal. Now proceed step-by-step, keeping your hope alive, keeping your goal in mind. Pull out your road map of where you have listed your goals for each of the ten (10) phases. That is the path to your dreams. You will feel great when you achieve all of the goals you want. Get started and make it happen. The world needs your greatness. We need people like you to help the world. So go out there and be a hero—save a life. Start with yours.

How to Reach Harvey Alston
BEST, INC.
Harvey Alston
2665 Mitzi Drive
Columbus, Ohio 43209
614/235–5411 Office
Call 24 hours, seven days a week.

WORKOUT GEAR

		Quantity	Amount	Indicate sizes S, M, L, XL
#118-A	"ATTITUDE" Pins - $9.95	_____	$ _____	
#118-B	"The Best" Lapel Pins - $9.95	_____	_____	
#119	"Be The Best" Coffee Mug - $5.00	_____	_____	
#101	Auburn Duo-Stripe Satin Baseball Jacket - $35.00	_____	_____	
#102	Cannon Royal Classic Robe - $35.00	_____	_____	
#103	"Be The Best" Hat - $9.95	_____	_____	
#104	T-Shirt, Black with White Letters - $9.95	_____	_____	
#105	Baggy Sweats, Black with White Letters - $20.00	_____	_____	
#106	Big Top Sweatshirt, Black with White Letters - $20.00	_____	_____	
#107	Baggy Shorts, Black with White Letters - $20.00	_____	_____	
#108	Baggy Shorts, White with Black Letters - $20.00	_____	_____	
#109	Big Top Sweatshirt, White with Black Letters - $20.00	_____	_____	
#110	Baggy Sweats, White with Black Letters - $20.00	_____	_____	
#111	"Tank Top", White with Black Letters - $9.95	_____	_____	
#112	Towel for Work Outs - $9.95	_____	_____	
#113	T-Shirt, White with Black Letters - $9.95	_____	_____	
#114	"Tank Top", Black with White Letters - $9.95	_____	_____	

Tapes and Books

		Quantity	Amount
#115	BE THE BEST Cassette Tape - $9.95	_____	$_____
	BE THE BEST Book - $16.95	_____	_____
	BLACK MALES Book - $16.95	_____	_____
Videocassettes:			
#116	"Be The Best" not pictured - $19.95	_____	_____
#117	"To Be Or Not To Be" - $19.95	_____	_____
		Totals:	$_____

Make Check or Money Order Payable To: Please send to:

Harvey Alston   Name _____

2665 Mitzi Drive   Address _____

Columbus, Ohio 43209–3263   City_____ State _____ Zip _____

614/235–411   Phone: _____

Be the Best Fitness

Item #101
Auburn Duo-Stripe Satin Baseball Jacket, Kasha Lined
100% Nylon Satin. White duo-stripe collar, cuffs, and band. Raglan sleeves. Snap front closure. Slash pockets. Water repellent.

Item #102
Cannon Royal Classic Robe
100% Cotton Terry Velour. Extra thick. Looped cotton terry inside, set-in sleeves, double belt loop, 2 patch pockets, 48 inches long. Individual poly bag. **One size fits all.**

Item #103
Be the Best Hat

Item #104
BEST by FRUIT OF THE LOOM®
Adult Heavyweight T-Shirt
50% Polyester/50% Cotton.
Taped neck. Generous cut. "T"-
Shirt, M, L, XL
Black with white letters

Item #105
Baggy Sweats
S, M, L, XL
Black with white letters

Item #106
Big Top Sweatshirt
M, L, XL
Black with white letters

Item #107
Baggy Shorts
M, L, XL
Black with white letters

Item #108
Baggy Shorts, 100% Cotton
S, M, L, XL
White with black letters

Item #109
Big Top Sweatshirt 100% Cotton
M, L, XL
White with black letters

Item #110
Baggy Sweats
S, M, L, XL
White with black letters

Item #111
Sport Shirt, Tank Top
Preshrunk 100% Cotton
S, M, L, XL
White with black letters

Item #112
Towel for Work Outs
One size only

Item #113
T-Shirt
White with black letters

Item #114
Tank Top
Black with white letters

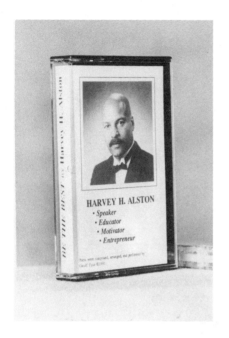

Item #115
Cassette Tape

1 hour "live" performance at St. Charles High School, Columbus Ohio.

The program featuring Harvey Alston with some of his greatest stories of motivation not found in his book. The background music was composed, arranged, and performed by his good friend, Geoff Tyus.

Great for those trips in your car when you need to be motivated.

Item #117
"To Be Or Not To Be"

You will feel like part of the audience when you watch this videocassette. The live performance at New Mexico Junior College was spellbinding. You can see Harvey Alston work his magic and feel your heart pound as the audience is moved to excitement. Glen McKay did a great job with the visual effects as he recorded this performance "live".

Great for classroom viewing.

Item #118A and #118B
Lapel Pins

Item #119
Coffee Mug

Recommended Reading

The Power of Positive Thinking, Norman Vincent Peale, New York: Fawcett, 1978.

Tough Times Never Last, But Tough People Do, Robert H. Schuller, Nashville: Thomas Nelson, 1983.

The Magic of Thinking Big, David J. Schwartz, St. Louis: Cornerstone, 1962.

Success Through A Positive Mental Attitude, Napoleon Hill and W. Clement Stone, New York: Pocket Books, 1977.

Seeds of Greatness, Denis Waitley, Ph.D., Old Tappan, New Jersey: Fleming H. Revell, 1983.

See You At The Top, Zig Ziglar, Gretna, LA: Pelican, 1975.

How To Win Friends and Influence People, Rev. Ed., Dale Carnegie, New York: Pocket Books, 1982.

Acres of Diamonds, Russell H. Conwell, Old Tappan, New Jersey: Fleming H. Revell, 1975.

The Aerobics Program for Total Well-Being, Kenneth Cooper, M.D., New York: M. Evans, 1982.

Life Is Tremendous, Charlie Jones, Wheaton: Tyndale House, 1981.

Psycho-Cybernetics, Maxwell Maltz, New York: Pocket Books, 1970.

The Greatest Miracle In The World, Og Mandino, New York: Bantam, 1977.

INDEX

Index of Worksheets